THE SENSORY CONNECTION PROGRAM

HANDBOOK

ACCOMPANYING MATERIALS TO THE SENSORY CONNECTION PROGRAM MANUAL

By

Karen M. Moore, OTR/L

Published by Therapro, Inc.

DISCLAIMER

Any program of physical activity has inherent risks and may result in injury. Not all exercise programs are suitable for all people. It is advised that participants in this program consult a physician or appropriate medical professional before starting. The information presented in this book is not intended to replace the advice of a doctor or therapist. The author, publisher and distributors of The Sensory Connection Program are not responsible for any illness or injury that may result from participation in this program.

Developmental Editor: Karen Conrad Weihrauch, Therapro, Inc.
Design and Art Direction: Dave Asselin
Copy Editor: Lorretta Holloway
Published by Therapro, Inc.
Movement Illustrations by Adam Pagano

Copyright © 2005 Karen M. Moore

Permission is granted to reproduce and distribute copies of the handouts, mini posters and worksheets contained in this book in limited quantities for non-commercial, educational use only. All copies must include the Copyright Notice.

Reproduction and distribution of the handouts, mini posters, and worksheets of this book for an entire institution and group of students or professionals is strictly prohibited.

Therapro, Inc.
225 Arlington Street
Framingham, MA 01702-8723
1-508-872-9494
1-800-257-5376
www.theraproducts.com

TABLE OF CONTENTS

PART 1	INTRODUCTION	1
PART 2	CHAPTER 2: TRAINING PACKET	3
PART 3	CHAPTER 3 (A, B, C): LEVEL I: SENSE-ABILITY TREATMENT - GROUP STAGES AND ACTIVITIES	19
PART 4	CHAPTER 4 (A, B): LEVEL II: COPING THROUGH THE SENSES - GROUP AND INDIVIDUAL TREATMENT	83
PART 5	CHAPTER 5: ENVIRONMENTAL SUPPORT	121

PART 1

INTRODUCTION

The *Sensory Connection Program Handbook* is used in conjunction with *The Sensory Connection Program Manual*. The purpose of having this separate handbook is to make all of the educational handouts, worksheets, directions, and activity sheets referred to in *The Sensory Connection Program* easily accessible to the leader. The Handbook chapters are organized to correspond to the Manual chapters. That is, all the materials referred to in Chapter 2 of the Manual are located in Part 2, Chapter 2 of the Handbook. Each Handout, Worksheet, and Activity in the Handbook has been assigned an identification number that corresponds to the chapter it is in, followed by a number indicating its sequence within the chapter. For example, a Handout in Chapter 2 that is the 7th item listed in that chapter is numbered 2.7.

Use The Sensory Connection Program Handbook:

- with the Manual. Open the Handbook to the Worksheets and Activities referred to in the Manual.

- to copy informational handouts for training staff, patients and care providers about the underlying concepts of *The Sensory Connection Program*.

- to design individual and group treatment sessions (also, offer the Handbook to staff members and students, so they can review options and activities for designing individual and group treatments).

- as a guide for treatment ideas. The beginning of each chapter in the Handbook lists all the activities within that chapter.

Copyright © 2005 Karen M. Moore

Copyright © 2005 Karen M. Moore

PART 2

CHAPTER 2: TRAINING PACKET

TRAINING OUTLINE *Handout* **2.1** 5

CALMING AND ALERTING CHARACTERISTICS
      OF SENSORY INPUT *Handout* **2.2** 7

SENSORY CONNECTION PROGRAM STRATEGIES FOR
      MENTAL HEALTH PROBLEMS *Handout* **2.3** 10

SYMPTOMS OF DISTRESS *Mini-Poster* **2.4** 14

PRECAUTIONS FOR PROTECTING PATIENT SAFETY *Handout* **2.5**. 15

PRECAUTIONS FOR PROTECTING STAFF AND
      CAREGIVER SAFETY *Handout* **2.6**. 16

SAFE SENSE *Mini-Poster* **2.7** 17

Copyright © 2005 Karen M. Moore

The Sensory Connection Program Training Outline

I. Introduction to the Sensory Systems and Deep Abdominal Breathing

    Materials: *Calming and Alerting Characteristics of Sensory Input* Handout (see 2.2)

        A. Overview of the Senses

        B. The Sense of Smell

        C. The Sense of Taste

        D. The Oral Motor Sense

        E. The Sense of Vision

        F. The Sense of Hearing

        G. The Sense of Touch

        H. The Sense of Proprioception

        I. The Vestibular Sense

        J. Abdominal Breathing

II. Sensory Strategies for Mental Health Problems

    Materials: *Sensory Connection Program Strategies for Mental Health Problems* Handout (see 2.3)

        A. Overview of How the Program Helps

        B. Helping with Stress

        C. Helping with Emotional Regulation

        D. Helping with Poor Reality Orientation

        E. Helping with Sensory Distortions

        F. Helping with Sensory Defensiveness

2.1 HANDOUT (page 2 of 2)

      G. Helping with Dissociation and Flashbacks

      H. Helping with Suicidality

      I. Helping with Self-injurious Behaviors

      J. Helping with Negative Thinking

      K. Helping with Disorganization

      L. Helping with Cognitive Problems

      M. Helping with Substance Abuse

III. Protecting Patient and Staff Safety

Materials: *Symptoms of Distress* Mini-Poster (see 2.4)

Precautions for Protecting Patient Safety Handout (see 2.5)

Precautions for Protecting Staff and Caregiver Safety Handout (see 2.6)

Safe Sense Mini-Poster (see 2.7)

      A. Patient Safety Considerations

          1. Recognizing Symptoms of Distress

          2. Medical Issues

          3. Cognitive Issues

          4. Emotional Issues

          5. Behavioral Issues

      B. Staff and Caregiver Safety

Copyright © 2005 Karen M. Moore

Calming and Alerting Characteristics of Sensory Input

GENERAL CHARACTERISTICS

CALMING	ALERTING
■ Mild/Soft	■ Strong/Pronounced
■ Slow	■ Fast paced
■ Rhythmic	■ Non-rhythmic
■ Simple	■ Complex
■ Familiar	■ Novel
■ Expected/Predictable	■ Surprising/Unpredictable
■ Soothing	■ Irritating
■ Low demand	■ High demand
■ Positive associations	■ Negative associations

SMELL SENSATIONS

CALMING	ALERTING
■ Soothing scented candle (apple pie or vanilla)	■ Candles with crisp strong scent (lemon or peppermint)
■ Mild fragrances	■ Strong fragrances
■ Scented bath powder	■ Perfume
■ Pleasant smell	■ Noxious odor
■ Cedar filled pillow or Potpourri	■ Room fragrance spray
■ Positive associations	■ Negative associations

TASTE SENSATIONS

CALMING	ALERTING
■ Mild	■ Strong or spicy
■ Sweet	■ Sour or bitter
■ Sweet hard candy	■ Lemon drop
■ Lollipop	■ Strong peppermints
■ Pleasant	■ Distasteful
■ Oatmeal and brown sugar	■ Chili
■ Apple juice	■ Lemonade
■ Sweet fruits like cherries and grapes	■ Pickles

Copyright © 2005 Karen M. Moore

ORAL MOTOR SENSATIONS

CALMING	ORGANIZING	ALERTING	BREATH SUPPORT
Sucking	*Chewy*	*Crunchy*	*Blowing*
■ Hard candy	■ Gum	■ Popcorn	■ Blowing pinwheel
■ Thick liquid through straw	■ Bagel	■ Pretzels	■ Whistling
■ Sweet orange slices	■ Gummy bears	■ Raw vegetables	■ Kazoo
■ Lollipop	■ Licorice sticks	■ Crunchy cereal	■ Blowing bubbles
	■ Dried fruits	■ Crushed ice	■ Abdominal breathing

VISUAL SENSATIONS

CALMING	ALERTING
■ Soft colors	■ Bright colors
■ Natural or dim lighting	■ Artificial or bright lighting
■ Serene paintings (such as Monet)	■ Modern Art (such as Picasso)
■ Pleasant scenery	■ Complex visual images
■ Flickering candle or campfire	■ Changing patterns of light
■ Watching fish in aquarium	■ Video game
■ Study something lovely such as a rose	■ Watching a frisky puppy
■ Bubble lamp	■ Rotary sprinkler
■ Clean and sparsely furnished room	■ Messy and cluttered room

AUDITORY SENSATIONS

CALMING	ALERTING
■ Soft, slow music	■ Offbeat, loud, quick paced music
■ Classical or New Age music	■ Rock music
■ Familiar background noise (fan)	■ Unfamiliar background noise (hammering, alarm clock)
■ Humming	■ Whistling
■ Singing quietly	■ Singing loudly
■ Simple, melodic	■ Changing sounds (city streets)
■ Repetitive sounds (ocean waves)	■ Hand held instruments
■ Rock waterfall	
■ Meditation tapes	

TOUCH SENSATIONS

CALMING (DEEP PRESSURE TOUCH)	ALERTING (LIGHT TOUCH)
■ Strong hugs ■ Firm touch on the shoulder ■ Using a heavy quilt or cover ■ Deep massage ■ Something heavy on the lap (sleeping cat) ■ Neutral warmth ■ Squeezing a stress ball ■ Foot roller ■ Use of hand lotions ■ Rubbing smooth stones or Chinese Balls in the hand ■ Beanbag tapping	■ Tickling ■ Light stroking ■ Feeling something prickly or squishy ■ Unfamiliar or unexpected touch ■ Something moving on lap (frisky puppy) ■ Cool room ■ Fiddling with a stress ball ■ Walking on grass ■ Snapping a rubber band on the wrist ■ Use of "fidget widgets"

PROPRIOCEPTIVE SENSATIONS

CALMING	ALERTING
■ Joint compression ■ Slow rhythmic movements ■ Heavy, sustained resistance ■ Walking ■ Weight lifting ■ Yoga ■ Tai chi ■ Pushing hands together or against a wall ■ Chair pushups ■ Lifting, carrying, pushing	■ Quick changes ■ Jerky movements ■ Jarring, changing activities ■ Jogging ■ Stepper machine ■ Aerobic exercise ■ Kick boxing ■ Jumping

VESTIBULAR SENSATIONS

CALMING	ALERTING
■ Rocking/Rocking chair ■ Riding in a car ■ Slow dancing ■ Swinging gently ■ Stationary activities – Chess ■ Walking ■ Slow head roles ■ Sitting on something sturdy & motionless ■ Glider	■ Squirming ■ Riding on a tractor ■ Fast dancing ■ Spinning quickly ■ Movement activities ■ Jogging ■ Quick movements of head ■ Sitting on therapy ball ■ Swing

Copyright © 2005 Karen M. Moore

Sensory Connection Program Strategies for Mental Health Problems

Stress

- Develop a stress management plan with help and support of care provider (*Worksheet* 4.7)

- Develop a personal stress management plan (*Worksheet* 4.7; *Handout* 4.15)

- Learn stress management skills (Level II: Coping Through the Senses Group *Topic* 6)

- Use movement and exercise and activities that provide strong sensory input (Sense-ability Group; *Handout* 4.20)

- Experience fun, success oriented activities and leisure possibilities in the Sense-ability Group

- Plan to participate daily in leisure activities and balance work, rest, and play (Level II: Coping Through the Senses Group *Topics* 9 & 10)

- Learn and practice deep abdominal breathing (*Worksheets* 4.22.1 & 4.22.2)

Emotional Regulation

- Identify sensory input that helps with calming (*Handout* 4.15)

- Develop a Sensory Kit for Calming (*Handout* 4.16)

- Learn to use calming sensory input (Level II: Coping Through the Senses Group *Topics* 1, 2, & 4)

- Develop an Alerting Snack Box (*Handouts* 4.17 & 4.18)

- Develop a Sensory Input Plan (Level II: Coping Through the Senses Group *Topic* 8)

Poor Reality Orientation

- Provide strong deep pressure and proprioceptive input (*Handout* 4.20)

- Participate in the Sense-ability Group designed to help with personal and environmental orientation

- Engage in simple work activities (making bed, folding laundry)

- Provide cues through environmental adaptations (*Handouts* 5.5, 5.6, 5.8)

Sensory Distortions

- Minimize aversive stimulation through environmental adjustments (*Handout* 4.19)
- Restrict patient to quiet area or own room
- Develop and use Safe Space (*Handout* 5.7)
- Use structured individual treatment using stages of Sense-ability Group

Sensory Defensiveness

- Recognize symptoms of sensory defensiveness (*Screening* 4.23.2)
- Follow the Acute Care Treatment Plan for Sensory Defensiveness (*Handout* 4.23.3)
- Eliminate aversive sensory stimulation (*Handout* 4.19)
- Plan for regular use of strong sensory stimulation to help normalize the sensory system (*Handout* 4.20)

Dissociation and Flashbacks

- Immediately use strong alerting sensory stimulation for grounding (*Handout* 4.8)
- Use calming sensory input once patient is grounded in reality (*Handout* 4.15)
- Improve recognition of mind and body responses and emotions (Level II: Coping Through the Senses Group *Topic* 3)
- Develop a repertoire of grounding strategies and develop a Perfume Canister (*Handout* 4.8)
- Learn coping strategies and coping strategies (Level II: Coping Through the Senses Group *Topics* 2, 5, & 7)

Suicidality

- Use calming sensory input (*Handout* 4.15)
- Use grounding techniques (*Handout* 4.8)
- Engage in leisure activities (*Worksheet* 4.11)

Self-injurious Behaviors

- Intervene early with calming sensory input (*Handout* 4.15)
- Provide regular use of strong sensory stimulation (*Handout* 4.20)
- Provide beanbag tapping on a regular basis several times a day (*Handout* 4.12)
- Develop a Sensory Kit for Calming (*Handout* 4.16)
- Utilize Safe Space (*Handout* 5.7)
- Develop and use a Sensory Room (*Handout* 5.4)
- Use sensory interventions for self-injurious behaviors (*Handout* 5.3)
- Use sensory strategies to avoid the use of restraints (*Handout* 5.2)

Negative Thinking

- Offer opportunities for successful experiences through the Sense-ability Group
- Encourage participation in leisure and enjoyable hobbies (*Worksheet* 4.11)

Disorganization

- Use activities that help with self awareness including beanbag tapping (*Handout* 4.12)
- Provide environmental support (*Handouts* 5.5 & 5.6)
- Provide sensory cues (*Handout* 5.9)
- Provide activities that provide strong, organizing sensory input (*Handout* 4.20)
- Involve in the Sense-ability Group which is designed to help with organization and cognitive support

Cognitive Problems

- Provide activities that are appropriate for patient cognitive level

- Use carefully chosen alerting activities to help with attention (*Handouts* 4.17 & 4.18)

- Use the body or sensory system (beanbag tapping) instead of mindfulness techniques (*Handout* 4.12)

- Involve in supportive Sense-ability Group

- Provide sensory cues and environmental adaptations (*Handout* 5.9)

Substance Abuse

- Explore suggestions for sober leisure and alternative ways to feel good and have fun (*Worksheet* 4.11)

- Develop a balance of work, rest, and play (*Worksheet* 4.10)

- Learn positive coping strategies (Level II: Coping Through the Senses Group *Topics* 1 & 2)

- Develop a plan for stress management (*Worksheet* 4.7)

Symptoms of Distress

Stop!!!!

These are signs that a person is having difficulty tolerating the activity

- ✔ Acting out
- ✔ Anxiety
- ✔ Excuses
- ✔ Confusion
- ✔ Irritability
- ✔ Resistance to activity
- ✔ Defensive behaviors
- ✔ Lightheadedness
- ✔ Increased perspiration
- ✔ Flushing or pallor
- ✔ Shortness of breath
- ✔ Over arousal
- ✔ Paranoia
- ✔ Fearful expression

Precautions for Protecting Patient Safety

Medical Precautions:

1. **Review the patient chart**, making note of any medical issues of concern for engaging in program activities. (Example: the medicine ball activity is a poor choice for patients with cardiac problems.)
2. **Note any medications** that can cause side effects or distress during activities. (Example: a patient taking meds that cause thirst should be encouraged to leave the group if necessary to obtain fluids.)
3. **Look at the communication board used by staff** prior to treatment and note any concerns or precautions regarding the current unit patients.
4. **Factor medical concerns into choices of activities** for group and individual treatment.
5. **Consult with the patient's primary care physician** whenever a stress management plan or home activity plan involves physical exertion to determine if movement, exercise, or heavy work activities is advisable.

Cognitive Precautions:

1. **Understand patient cognitive capacities** using the Allen Cognitive Level Screening (ACLS).
2. **Assign patients with serious cognitive difficulties to Level I treatment**, which is more supportive and helps to compensate for cognitive difficulties.
3. **Warn caregivers of potential problems** due to cognitive difficulties because the person in their care might do unsafe things he or she would never do ordinarily.

Emotional Precautions:

1. **Become familiar with a patient's background**, presenting problem, and emotional issues to make interventions effective and to avoid the possibility of embarrassing the patient with specific topics or activities.
2. **Avoid triggers** that remind the patient of past traumatic experiences.
3. **Remind patients that they can feel free to leave a group** if something upsets them or causes strong negative associations.

Behavioral Precautions:

1. **Watch for early signs of agitation** and control the situation as early as possible.
2. **Allow the patient a wide range of personal space**.
3. **Offer reassurance with a calm voice**; some patients' act out when they are frightened.
4. **Have a plan in place in the event of a crisis situation**. Violent behaviors should never be handled without assistance.
5. **Contract with the patient for safety and appropriate behavior** prior to treatment if a patient has a history of problematic behaviors. The therapist and patient should decide on a code word or signal that can be used if problems arise.

2.6 HANDOUT

Precautions for Protecting Staff and Caregiver Safety

1. **Consult with other staff members or the patient chart to determine if there is a potential for danger** before initiating treatment,

2. **Respect personal space.** Sensory treatment modalities are very personal and sometimes involve touch and close personal contact.

3. **NEVER touch a patient without obtaining permission,** even if it seems likely that the person would enjoy an activity.

4. **Respect a patient's decision not to try a particular activity**; determine the source of reticence before further encouragement.

5. **Pay close attention to symptoms of distress and to non-verbal communication** of anger, hostility, distrust, agitation, or loss of self-control. Treatment should be postponed if safety is at risk.

6. **Avoid surprises.** Prepare patients for activities by describing them ahead of time so that patients can leave or seek help if they are uncomfortable with the activity.

7. **Dress with safety in mind.** Avoid large hoop earrings or jewelry that can be grabbed. Avoid any clothing that is skimpy or that can be construed as being sexually provocative. Avoid wearing strong colognes.

8. **Position yourself to escape** through a door in case a patient becomes assaultive when evaluating or providing individual treatment to an unknown patient.

9. **Invite patients to walk beside you,** not behind you.

SAFE SENSE

1. Assess patient safety prior to treatment.

2. Respect personal space.

3. Always ask permission to touch someone.

4. Respect a patient's decision not to participate in an activity.

5. Watch for upsetting sensory stimuli and symptoms of distress.

6. Avoid surprises; prepare a patient ahead of time.

7. Avoid loud or provocative clothing and strong colognes.

8. Position yourself to escape through a door.

9. Invite patients to walk beside you not behind you.

Copyright © 2005 Karen M. Moore

PART 3

CHAPTER 3: LEVEL I SENSE-ABILITY TREATMENT GROUP STAGES AND ACTIVITIES

SENSE-ABILITY GROUP PROTOCOL *Handout* 3.1 23
OUTLINE OF STAGES OF THE SENSE-ABILITY GROUP *Handout* 3.2 25
BASIC SUPPLY LIST FOR THE SENSE-ABILITY GROUP *Handout* 3.3 26
PLANNING A SENSE-ABILITY GROUP *Mini Poster* 3.4 27
SENSE-ABILITY GROUP STAGE I:
 THE ATTENDING STAGE *Activity Directions* 3.5 28
  Activity 1: Scented Candles 3.5.1 28
  Activity 2: Ribbon Wand 3.5.2 28
  Activity 3: Jacob's Ladder 3.5.3 29
  Activity 4: What's that Sound? 3.5.4 29
  Activity 5: Got Beans? 3.5.5 30
  Activity 6: Bop-It or Simon 3.5.6 30
  Activity 7: Balancing Bird, Eraser, or Plastic
   Ruler on Fingertip 3.5.7 31
  Activity 8: Colored Glasses 3.5.8 31
  Activity 9: What's that Smell? 3.5.9 32
  Activity 10: Heavy Duty Dogs 3.5.10 32
  Activity 11: Slinky 3.5.11 33
  Activity 12: Chinese Balls or Smooth Stones 3.5.12 33
  Activity 13: Kaleidoscopes 3.5.13 33
  Activity 14: Guatemalan Worry Dolls 3.5.14 34
  Activity 15: Gifts of Nature 3.5.15 34
  Activity 16: Scented Hand Creams 3.5.16 34
  Activity 17: Pinwheels 3.5.17 35
  Activity 18: Hoberman Sphere 3.5.18 35
  Activity 19: Tea Time 3.5.19 36
  Activity 20: Music and Instruments 3.5.20 36
  Activity 21: Pin Art 3.5.21 37
  Activity 22: Spinner 3.5.22 37

Copyright © 2005 Karen M. Moore

SENSE-ABILITY GROUP STAGE II: THE MOVING AND BREATHING STAGE *Activity Directions* 3.6 38
    Activity 1: Start Up 3.6.1 39
    Activity 2: Rock and Roll 3.6.2 39
    Activity 3: Trunk Turns 3.6.3 40
    Activity 4: Neck Rolls 3.6.4 40
    Activity 5 Chin Up 3.6.5 41
    Activity 6: Lookout Neck Stretch 3.6.6 41
    Activity 7: Triceps Stretch 3.6.7 42
    Activity 8: Cat Stretch 3.6.8 42
    Activity 9: Apple Picker 3.6.9 43
    Activity 10: Arm Lengthener 3.6.10 43
    Activity 11 Wing It 3.6.11 44
    Activity 12: Cross Your Heart 3.6.12 44
    Activity 13: Uptight Penguin 3.6.13 45
    Activity 14: Fence Painter 3.6.14 45
    Activity 15: High Hand Shake 3.6.15 46
    Activity 16: Hand Press 3.6.16 46
    Activity 17: Foot Flexor 3.6.17 47
    Activity 18: Heels and Toes 3.6.18 47
    Activity 19: Marching in Place 3.6.19 48
    Activity 20: Foot Leader 3.6.20 48
    Activity 21: Glider/Slider 3.6.21 49
    Activity 22: Beach Ball Circles 3.6.22 49
    Activity 23: Peacock Peck 3.6.23 50
    Activity 24: Finger Manipulations 3.6.24 50
    Activity 25: Hand Massage 3.6.25 51
    Activity 26: Wave/Swim 3.6.26 51
    Activity 27: Palm Up/Palm Down 3.6.27 52
    Activity 28: Standard Deep Breathing 3.6.28 53
    Activity 29: Deep Breathing with a Sigh 3.6.29 53
    Examples of Movement Routines *Mini Poster* 3.6.30 54

SENSE-ABILITY GROUP STAGE III: THE CONVERSING STAGE *Activity Directions* 3.7 55

SENSE-ABILITY GROUP STAGE IV: THE SENSING STAGE *Activity Directions* 3.8 56
    Activity 1: Beanbag Tapping 3.8.1 56
    Activity 2: Medicine Ball 3.8.2 56
    Activity 3: Exercise Band Rowing 3.8.3 57
    Activity 4: Parachute Games 3.8.4 57

**SENSE-ABILITY GROUP STAGE V: THE ACTING AND
INTERACTING STAGE** *Activity Directions* **3.9** 58
   Activity 1: Indoor Bocce 3.9.1 58
   Activity 2: The Name Game 3.9.2 59
   Activity 3: Balloon Game 3.9.3 59
   Activity 4: Floor Basketball 3.9.4 60
   Activity 5: Indoor Basketball 3.9.5 60
   Activity 6: Velcro Target Games 3.9.6 61
   Activity 7: Rubber Tipped Darts 3.9.7 61
   Activity 8: Reacher Toss 3.9.8 62
   Activity 9: Ring Toss 3.9.9 62
   Activity 10: Horseshoes 3.9.10 63
   Activity 11: The Bucket Game 3.9.11 63
   Activity 12: Game Center Basketball 3.9.12 64
   Activity 13: Indoor Golf 3.9.13 64
   Activity 14: Dice and Hoops 3.9.14 64
   Activity 15: Koosh Woosh Frisbee Rings and Cones 3.9.15 65
   Activity 16: Dice and Therapy Ball 3.9.16 65
   Activity 17: Indoor Shuffleboard 3.9.17 66

**SENSE-ABILITY GROUP STAGE VI: THE LEARNING
STAGE** *Activity Directions* **3.10** 67
   Activity 1: Gestures 3.10.1 67
   Activity 2: Goal Setting Game 3.10.2 68
   Activity 3: Safety and Leisure Words 3.10.3 69
   Activity 4: "Who Would You Call?" Game 3.10.4 71
   Activity 5: Emotion Games 3.10.5 72
   Activity 6: Supports Game 3.10.6 73
   **Activity 7: Sports Matching Game/Picture
               Matching Game 3.10.7** 74
   Activity 8: Riddles 3.10.8 75
   Activity 9: "Getting to Know You" Game 3.10.9 76
   Activity 10: Music Activities 3.10.10 77
   Activity 11: Assertiveness Game 3.10.11 78
   Activity 12: Discharge Planning Game 3.10.12 79
   Activity 13: Social Skills Game 3.10.13 80
   Activity 14: "Using Sensory Input" Game 3.10.14 81

Level I:
Sense-Ability Group Protocol

Description/Purpose of Group:

This group is highly structured as well as non-competitive and provides an accepting environment to help patients engage in movements and sensory experiences that are also physically, cognitively, and socially challenging. The ultimate goal is that the patient will be able to successfully organize adaptive responses to self, others, and the environment.

Goals of the Group:

Specific goals from this list will be identified in the patient's treatment plan. Patients will:

1. improve sensory awareness of self, others, and the environment.

2. increase self-control.

3. learn healthy methods for reducing stress, tension, and anxiety including exercise, relaxation methods, leisure activities, and the value of a balanced routine.

4. increase attention, reality orientation, and problem solving.

5. improve energy, motivation, and activity tolerance.

6. increase self-esteem through improved body image and success oriented experiences.

7. increase social skills, social conduct, as well as the ability to appropriately express feelings and emotions.

8. increase coping skills, use of supports, and health maintenance strategies.

Membership of Group:

Group size is flexible but this group can accommodate from 12-14 patients on a regular basis.

Patients who will benefit the most from participation in this group score between 3.0 and 4.8 on the Allen Cognitive Level Screening (ACLS). Patients with the following symptoms will also benefit: poor attention, poor memory skills, confusion, disorganization, poor reality orientation, psychosis, sensory issues, impaired social skills, poor behavioral control, impulsiveness, mania, anhedonia, and psychomotor retardation (delayed motor responses sometimes seen in severe depression). This group can sometimes be appropriate for patients with extreme anxiety and for patients who have experienced emotional trauma. Geriatric patients on a psychiatric unit often benefit more from this group regardless of their ACL.

Copyright © 2005 Karen M. Moore

3.1 HANDOUT (page 2 of 2)

Members are encouraged to remain for the entire group, but the group is designed to accommodate fringe participants (patients who sit off to the side of the group but are aware of the group activities) as well as those patients with short attention spans and limited endurance for activity who may have to leave the group. Members can leave if necessary, they are encouraged to return if possible.

Location and Frequency:

Conduct this 60-minute group daily, if possible. The location should be a large room that is comfortable, easily accessible to patients, and brightly lit.

Group Leadership:

Ideally co-lead the group with two therapists, staff members, or students, unless the group is unusually small (5 or less patients). All leaders should receive training on sensory input, conduction of the group, and safety.

Precautions:

Provide supervision of activities to assure proper body mechanics and safe techniques. Exercises that involve holding and arms raised over the head should be avoided for any patients with cardiac problems. Grade or adapt the exercises for patients with physical limitations. Movements of the exercise routine should be slow and rhythmic to avoid strain and the stretch reflex. Most of the movements are performed in the sitting position to accommodate a wide range of physical and mental incapacities. Equipment and target games are chosen carefully according to the acuity and safety status of the group members.

Methods:

This group consists of a short welcome, six stages, and a brief closing. Patients and staff sit in a circle of chairs in a large bright room. Everyone is encouraged to participate, including staff and guests. Co-leaders bring necessary equipment to the room including the tape player, tapes, target games, and props.

An outline for the group stages follows as a separate sheet so it can be copied for easy reference.

HANDOUT 3.2

Stages of the Sense-Ability Group

■ **Welcoming** – 1 minute

    Welcome patients as they enter the group area. Give a brief explanation of the group.

■ **Stage 1: The Attending Stage** – 8 minutes

    Stimulation of the external senses. Pass an item with sensory interest around to be examined. Ask patients to comment on their personal experience of the smell, taste, auditory or visual characteristics, or texture.

■ **Stage 2: The Moving and Breathing Stage** – 10 minutes

    Music/Movement Routine. Lead a gentle stretching and exercise routine to the tune of soft and flowing music. The rhythmic movements and breathing exercises are designed to break up tension and to foster self-awareness.

■ **Stage 3: The Conversing Stage** – 2 minutes

    Recognition and Comments. Acknowledge each patient by name and ask for his or her comments on the relaxation experience.

■ **Stage 4: The Sensing Stage** – 4 minutes

    Intense Stimulation of the Internal Senses. This section uses some form of strong proprioceptive, vestibular, or deep pressure touch input that is designed to promote body awareness, organization, and self-control. The activity that is most commonly used is Beanbag Tapping.

■ **Stage 5: The Acting/Interacting Stage** – 16 minutes

    Target Games. Have patients play two target games with graded challenges. These activities test adaptive responses, ability to follow directions, perceptual and sequencing skills, and social awareness and conduct.

■ **Stage 6: The Learning Stage** – 18 minutes

    Skill Building Component. Use games and props to teach patients coping and ADL skills. A multi-sensory approach, role modeling, and repetition are utilized.

■ **Closing** – 1 minute

    Briefly review pertinent group experiences and reinforce the educational concepts. Thank everyone for coming to the group and remind them of the time and place that the group will be held again.

Copyright © 2005 Karen M. Moore

3.3 HANDOUT

Basic Supply List for the Setup of a Sense-ability Group

Resources for supplies can be found in the Appendix A of the Manual.

MATERIALS FOR STAGE I – AWARENESS STAGE

- Slinky
- Scented candles
- Scented hand creams
- Old time toys (Jacob's Ladder/Spinner)
- Bop-it or Simon
- Herbal teas and carafe
- Kaleidoscopes
- Heavy-duty dog
- Ribbon wand

MATERIALS FOR STAGE II – MOVING AND BREATHING STAGE

- 3 or more different audiotapes or compact disks of soothing, rhythmic music
- Tape recorder/CD player

MATERIALS FOR STAGE IV – SENSING STAGE

- Beanbags (Approximately 4" enough for all patients)
- Heavy Duty Exercise Band (4 loops made of 4' lengths)
- Medicine Ball (optional)
- Parachute (optional)

MATERIALS FOR STAGE V – ACTING/INTERACTING STAGE

- Ring toss
- Dart game
- Horseshoes
- 3 colorful plastic buckets
- File cards
- Soft balls including Koosh balls
- Basketball game
- Balloons
- Disk-O-Bocce
- 6" Dice
- 2 plastic 24" hoops

MATERIALS FOR STAGE VI – LEARNING STAGE

- Poster board or foam board
- Bright file cards
- Permanent Marker
- Clear contact paper or laminate
- Colored coding stickers
- Beanbags and Koosh balls

Copyright © 2005 Karen M. Moore

Planning a Sense-ability Group

Begin planning the Sense-ability Group by reviewing the treatment goals and problems and strengths of the patients. Then choose activities and equipment for each of the Six Stages. The following list can be used as a quick guide for selecting activities.

Stage 1 – Awareness Stage

Choose an item with sensory interest, such as a kaleidoscope.

Stage 2 - Moving and Breathing Stage

Select an audiotape, for example, a classical tape.

Stage 4 - Sensing Stage

Choose an activity that provides intense sensory stimulation, such as beanbag tapping.

Stage 5 – Acting/Interacting Stage

Select two target games, one being more challenging, such as ring toss and a basketball game.

Stage 6 – Learning Stage

Choose a game according to the needs and abilities of the particular group of patients, for example the Goal Setting Game.

3.5 ACTIVITY DIRECTIONS (page 1 of 10)

SENSE-ABILITY GROUP

Stage I: The Attending Stage

Time: 8 minutes

Choose ONE activity per session

3.5.1	ACTIVITY 1 SCENTED CANDLES
MODALITY	Smell
MATERIALS	Four scented candles with a strong identifiable aroma such as vanilla, pine, mint, lavender, or cinnamon. Candles in small jars with lids keep their aroma longer. Keep track of scents of candles by color, but cover or remove identification of scent on the label.
DIRECTIONS	Pass candles one at a time to patients and ask them try to guess the scents. The candle colors and the group's consensus of the scent can be written on a blackboard and then checked against the color key.
DISCUSSION	What are your favorite scents? Which scents do you find calming? Which scents help to make you feel more alert or pay better attention?

3.5.2	ACTIVITY 2 RIBBON WAND
MODALITY	Vision
MATERIALS	A ribbon wand. This is a long colored satin ribbon, 9 or more feet in length that is attached to a wooden dowel or stick. Cheerleaders and gymnasts sometimes use them and they are sometimes called ribbon sticks or ribbon twirls. A ribbon ball and ribbon hoops are very similar. Small versions are available or can be created so that each person in the group has one. To make a ribbon wand, one or more four-foot colorful ribbons are attached to a one-foot dowel; a button or ring can be substituted for the wand.
DIRECTIONS	Ask patients to take turns swirling and moving the ribbon stick to create different patterns. If all patients have a ribbon wand, they can follow movements together to the flow of music. Patients can volunteer to lead the motions.
DISCUSSION	What else do you associate with the ribbon (e.g., gymnasts using ribbons, rainbows, kites, parades)? What other sensory feelings do you get using the ribbon wand (e.g., feeling a breeze, sound)?

Copyright © 2005 Karen M. Moore

3.5.3 ACTIVITY 3 JACOB'S LADDER

MODALITY	Vision
MATERIALS	Jacob's Ladder. This is an old fashioned toy that consists of 6 small flat blocks connected together in a row with ribbons.
DIRECTIONS	Demonstrate the use of the item holding the top block between the index finger and thumb and then tilting it forward toward the side with ribbons until the block below drops to the bottom of the interlocked row of blocks. Manipulating the toy requires problem solving.
DISCUSSION	What other old time toys does this bring to mind (e.g., yoyos, hula-hoops, paddle ball)?

3.5.4 ACTIVITY 4 WHAT'S THAT SOUND?

MODALITY	Hearing
MATERIALS	Plastic bottles or eggs filled with various items that make distinguishable sounds such as rice, pennies, jellybeans, nuts, macaroni, and paper clips. To keep track of what is in each egg, make a master list with the color of the plastic eggs and their contents.
DIRECTIONS	List the items in the eggs on the blackboard as a visual cue. Have patients take turns shaking the eggs and guessing the contents. Write the group member's answers on the board and compare them to the master list.
DISCUSSION	What characteristics helped to identify the contents (e.g., size, amount, weight)?

Copyright © 2005 Karen M. Moore

3.5.5 ACTIVITY 5 GOT BEANS?

MODALITY	Taste
MATERIALS	A container of jellybeans. Gourmet jellybeans work best because of the variety of flavors. The jellybean package usually gives a key to the flavors.
DIRECTIONS	Using a gloved hand, pass out one jellybean to each patient. Instruct them to note the color carefully and then to suck or slowly chew the candy while trying to determine the flavor. Check key to verify flavor. Repeat with several more jellybeans. Flavors can be written on the blackboard as a cue for identification.
DISCUSSION	Is the taste sweet or sour? Describe the taste? Does it remind you of anything? If you ate a few of these, could this taste be strong enough to keep you alert?

3.5.6 ACTIVITY 6 BOP-IT OR SIMON

MODALITY	Hearing
MATERIALS	Bop-It. This is a hand held musical toy by Parker Brothers. It gives commands to "pull", "twist" or "bop" and the player tries to follow the commands. Simon is a hand held toy by Milton Bradley. It has four areas that light with corresponding sounds. The player tries to repeat a sequence of sounds. A new Simon is available that has multiplayer games.
DIRECTIONS	Have patients take turns playing with the fast paced musical games. Bop-It can be played with two players, one twisting and bopping and the other pulling according to the commands. Bop-It also has a sequence that can be used by a group. Simon is less demanding and noisy and tests ability to follow auditory sequences.
DISCUSSION	Did you find this activity fun, frustrating, or both? What did you like about it? Did you have any strategies that helped with your success?

3.5.7 ACTIVITY 7 BALANCING BIRD, ERASER OR PLASTIC RULER ON FINGERTIP

MODALITY	Vision, touch
MATERIALS	"Balancing bird." This is usually made of hard plastic and is sometimes painted to look like an eagle. The wings are weighted and the bird balances easily on the fingertip. A large pink eraser, a plastic ruler, or even a peacock feather can be a substitute.
DIRECTIONS	Have patients take turns to balance the item on the fingertip. Make it more difficult by having players move the finger, transfer the item to their opposite index finger, or transfer the item to a peer.
DISCUSSION	What makes the items balance easily? How does this compare to keeping your balance while standing on a stool?

3.5.8 ACTIVITY 8 COLORED GLASSES

MODALITY	Vision
MATERIALS	Six pairs of sunglasses or colored glasses with lenses of various colors. Many inexpensive varieties are available ranging from amber to rose to gray.
DIRECTIONS	Have patients take turns trying on the various glasses and discuss which colors they find comfortable or uncomfortable.
DISCUSSION	What was your favorite colored lens? Do the colored glasses change the color of items in the room? Do any of the colored lenses make you feel happy or dismal? Do you have a preference in lens color in sunglasses?

Copyright © 2005 Karen M. Moore

3.5.9 ACTIVITY 9 WHAT'S THAT SMELL?

MODALITY	Smell
MATERIALS	Set of scented crayons or markers.
DIRECTIONS	Patients scribble with the scented crayons or markers on small pieces of paper. Pass the scribbled scented papers around and ask the patients to guess the smells. Record the guesses of the colors and corresponding scents on the blackboard and then compare to the key on the crayon or marker box. Make the activity easier by listing the scents on the blackboard ahead of time.
DISCUSSION	Is the smell food-like or non-food? Is it sweet or acrid or musty? Is it a smell you like? What smell perks you up and makes you feel more alert? What smell gives you a calm peaceful feeling? What smells do you dislike and avoid?

3.5.10 ACTIVITY 10 HEAVY DUTY DOGS

MODALITY	Touch
MATERIALS	A large realistic stuffed dog or cat that is made heavy by replacing the stuffing with seed corn (less expensive than popcorn) available at feed and grain stores. A slit is made along a seam on the bottom of the animal and most of the stuffing is pulled out except for the tips of the paws and tail. Once the stuffing is replaced, the opening is hand sewn. A large dog can be made to weigh about 8 – 10 pounds.
DIRECTIONS	Pass the animal to patients and ask them to comment on the weight and feel of the dog.
DISCUSSION	Can you guess the weight of the dog? Do you like the feeling of the heavy animal on your lap? Do you find it calming to stroke the animal? Have you ever had a pet that you enjoyed? What else could you set on your lap to give that calming feeling?

3.5.11 ACTIVITY 11 SLINKY

MODALITY	Vision, touch
MATERIALS	Plastic slinky.
DIRECTIONS	Have patients take turns shifting the Slinky from hand to hand or manipulating it in another manner.
DISCUSSION	How does it feel when you move the slinky from hand to hand? Do you find it relaxing? Do you remember the slinky advertisement song? Can you remember any other classic toys (e.g., yoyo, hula hoop, Frisbee)?

3.5.12 ACTIVITY 12 CHINESE BALLS OR SMOOTH STONES

MODALITY	Touch
MATERIALS	Chinese Iron Balls. This set of shiny balls is usually sold in a fabric-covered box; they are also called Chinese Therapy Balls. Some make a chiming sound when rolled in the hand. A nice substitution for Chinese Balls is two small smooth stones from the beach or nature store.
DIRECTIONS	Have patients take turns manipulating the stones or iron balls in their hands. The feeling is meant to be calming.
DISCUSSION	American Indians used stones as "worry beads." If you found this activity calming, how could you use it in daily life (e.g., keep stones in the pocket to manipulate while walking or in the drawer of a desk to take out when thinking or taking a break)?

3.5.13 ACTIVITY 13 KALEIDOSCOPES

MODALITY	Vision
MATERIALS	A variety of kaleidoscopes.
DIRECTIONS	Ask patients to take turns looking through the kaleidoscopes.
DISCUSSION	Describe what you see in the kaleidoscope. What makes the colors and shapes change? Which one do you prefer? Which one is most complex? Which one is most colorful?

Copyright © 2005 Karen M. Moore

3.5.14 ACTIVITY 14 GUATEMALAN WORRY DOLLS

MODALITY	Vision
MATERIALS	Worry Dolls. These are tiny little dolls in ethnic costume that are made in Guatemala. They usually come in a small bag or tiny basket. According to the legend that comes with the dolls, children in Guatemala assign a worry to each doll and then place them under their pillow at night. When they awake, the worry is gone. Buttons or any small objects can be used to represent the dolls.
DIRECTIONS	Introduce the dolls and explain the legend. Pass the Worry Dolls around for patients to examine.
DISCUSSION	What worries would you assign to the dolls? Wouldn't it be nice if worries could be gotten rid of so easily? Give alternative ways of dealing with worries.

3.5.15 ACTIVITY 15 GIFTS OF NATURE

MODALITY	Vision, smell, touch
MATERIALS	Seashells, herbs, plants, flowers, pinecones, or other natural items.
DIRECTIONS	Pass nature items around for patients to examine, smell, and touch.
DISCUSSION	Describe some characteristics of the item (e.g., soft, prickly, colorful, aromatic). Does an item bring up a favorite activity or memory (e.g., going to the ocean, walking in the woods, gardening)?

3.5.16 ACTIVITY 16 SCENTED HAND CREAMS

MODALITY	Smell, touch
MATERIALS	Six containers of hand creams of varying scents. One should be scentless if possible for people with allergies. Include one that men would enjoy (sun tan lotion).
DIRECTIONS	Invite patients to smell the scents and to choose one to use for a hand massage. Demonstrate doing a thorough hand massage including a gentle pulling (traction) on the fingers at the end.
DISCUSSION	What are your favorite fragrances? When was the last time you paid attention to your hands? Does the hand massage feel good? How could you incorporate it into your daily routine?

3.5.17 ACTIVITY 17 PINWHEELS

MODALITY	Vision, respiration
MATERIALS	A variety of interesting pinwheels. Try to include the one that looks like a bird with spinning wings.
DIRECTIONS	Pass the pinwheels around the group and have patients take turns puffing on the pinwheels to make them turn. Encourage players to take as deep a breath as possible and blow out slowly and with a gentle even force.
DISCUSSION	Where is the best place to blow on the pinwheel to make it turn faster? Do the pinwheels bring up any particular associations or memories? Are you able to take a deep breath? Do you have any problems with breathing? If so are these problems being addressed?

3.5.18 ACTIVITY 18 HOBERMAN SPHERE

MODALITY	Vision, touch
MATERIALS	The mini size Hoberman Sphere expands from 5 ½" to 12." It is a colorful unfolding structure based on a unique geometric design.
DIRECTIONS	Have patients take turns tossing the sphere to one another and manipulating the sphere to make it expand and contract. If a player holds the sphere by one of the connecting square braces and tosses it, the sphere usually expands or contracts in the air.
DISCUSSION	What associations do you make with this sphere (e.g., geometric designs, space station, atom)?

Copyright © 2005 Karen M. Moore

3.5.19 ACTIVITY 19 TEA TIME

MODALITY	Smell, taste
MATERIALS	Three distinct flavors of herbal tea (examples: currant, lemon, and vanilla flavored teas or raspberry, cinnamon, and orange flavored teas). Pan or container to heat the water on the stove or in the microwave. 3 Carafes. Sugar and a sugar substitute. Hot cups. Plastic spoons or stirrers.
DIRECTIONS	Three flavors of tea are made up in carafes using three tea bags in each one. Have patients take turns smelling all three teas. Ask them to decide on one tea they would like to taste. A small amount of that tea is served in hot cups. Sugar and sugar substitute are offered.
DISCUSSION	Do you like the tea? Is it a strong or weak flavor? Does it taste like it smells? What pleasant memories do you associate with the smells? Do you have a favorite kind of tea besides the ones offered today?

3.5.20 ACTIVITY 20 MUSIC AND INSTRUMENTS

MODALITY	Hearing
MATERIALS	Audiotape or compact disk of some rhythmic music like multicultural music. Simple inexpensive instruments such as castanets, maracas, or rhythm sticks. Other instruments can also be used including cluster bells, tambourine, finger cymbals, triangle, or bongo drum.
DIRECTIONS	Ask patients to choose an instrument. Have them follow along with the beat of a musical audiotape.
DISCUSSION	What is your favorite instrument? Have you ever played an instrument? What type of music do you like?

3.5.21 ACTIVITY 21 PIN ART

MODALITY	Vision, touch
MATERIALS	A pin art toy, also called an image-maker. This consists of hundreds of blunted pins held in a structure in such a way that it gives a 3-D relief image of things that are pressed against it, such as a hand.
DIRECTIONS	Patients take turns making images. The easiest way is to hold the structure pin side up against the palm, which is turned upwards and then flipping the gadget over to see the image of the hand formed by the pins.
DISCUSSION	How do the pins feel to you?

3.5.22 ACTIVITY 22 SPINNER

MODALITY	Vision, hearing
MATERIALS	A spinner is an old time toy. It is colorful, and makes an interesting whirling sound. Handmade versions are sometimes is available at craft shops or fairs. Using the spinner properly involves problem solving. The spinner also makes an interesting whirling sound.
DIRECTIONS	Demonstrate using the gadget. Have patients take turns with it by holding the bottom ring and quickly pushing a bead up the braided wire that sets a spinner in motion. Have patients take turns with it.
DISCUSSION	What other objects or memories does the spinner bring to mind (e.g., top or carnival ride)? How would you describe the sound?

Copyright © 2005 Karen M. Moore

… 3.6 ACTIVITY DIRECTIONS (page 1 of 16)

SENSE-ABILITY GROUP

Stage II: The Moving and Breathing Stage

Time: 10 minutes

Choose 20 MOVEMENTS per session.

Begin by having calm music playing on an audiotape or CD

MOVEMENT EXERCISES	
DIRECTIONS	Guide the patients through a movement routine made up of approximately 20 of the following 27 movements. Vary the selected exercises and their sequence. Gross motor movements should precede fine motor movements of the hands and fingers. A common sequence is to begin with gross movements of the head and trunk, followed by movements of shoulders and arms, and then feet and legs. End with fine motor movements including hand and finger exercises. Examples of routines are offered as a Mini-Poster 3.3.30 in this Handbook.

The movements of this Stage need to be simple and non-threatening, as well as gentle and flowing. Rhythmic movement patterns are essential. If the movement involves a stretch, have patients hold it for approximately four seconds or to the count of four. Avoid quick stretches because they disrupt the calming effect of the sensory input. Do not have patients with cardiac problems participate in movements that involve resistance and holding patterns. During the exercise movements, exhale upon exertion. Relax and breathe between repetitions; remind patients to do so. Most movements are repeated a total of three times. Make the movement routine positive. Encourage patients to follow along with all of the exercises that they are comfortable doing and to omit those that cause pain or distress. It is more important that they relax and move in a comfortable fashion than it is that they follow the leader exactly.

A rationale for each of the exercises is provided in parentheses following the description of the movement. |

3.6.1 START UP

Begin by instructing patients to uncross legs and to put feet on the floor and hands on thighs. Remind patients not to perform movements that are painful or inordinately uncomfortable.

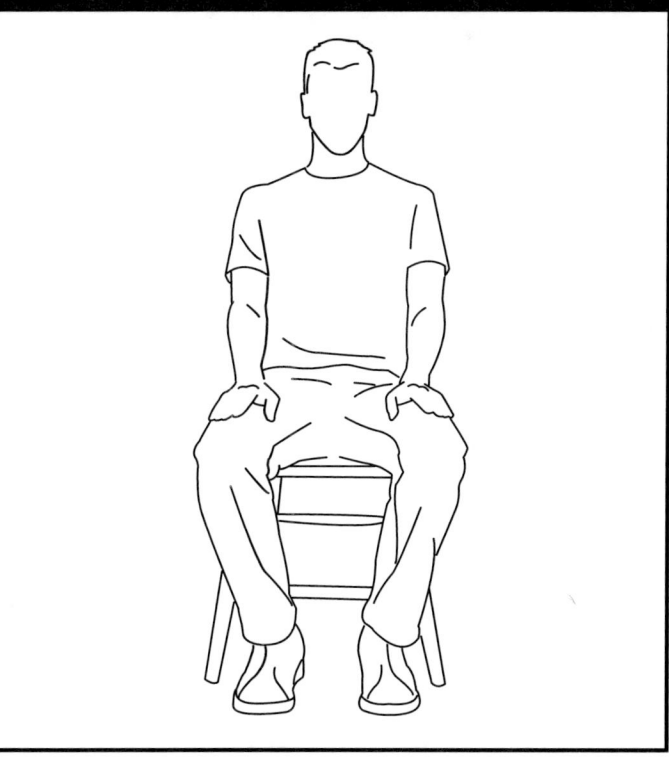

3.6.2 ROCK AND ROLL

Begin rocking side to side, gently, slowly 6X. Next start rocking around in a circle, rotating from the hips, 3X in one direction and then reverse and go 3X in the opposite direction. (Provides vestibular input, trunk stability, whole body focus, crossing midline, and stimulates spinal cord and fluid.)

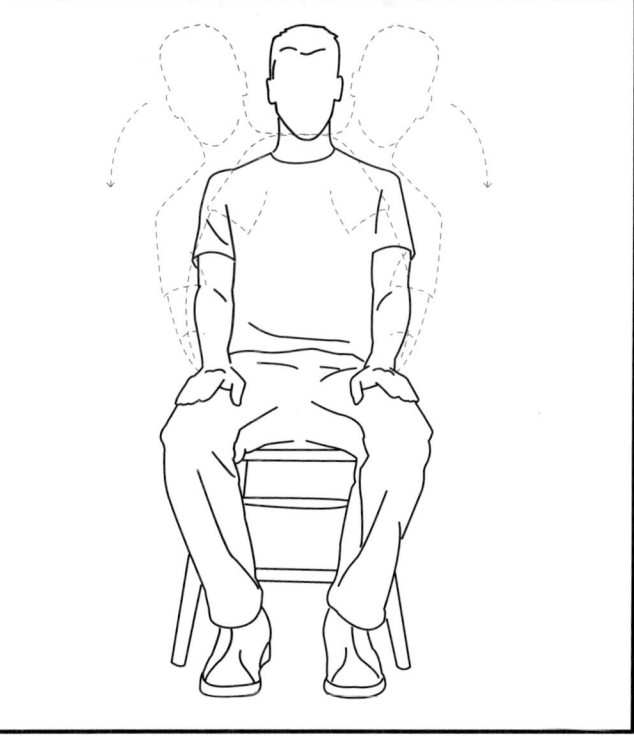

Copyright © 2005 Karen M. Moore

3.6.3 TRUNK TURNS

Interlace fingers of both hands and place them on the top of the head giving very gentle pressure. Turn slowly in one direction, twisting at the waist, until a gentle stretch is felt. Turn slowly to face forward again and then turn in the other direction until a stretch is felt. Repeat 2x. (Unlocks the spine, breaks up tension, gives proprioception to neck and hip joints, input is calming.)

3.6.4 NECK ROLLS

Drop head forward and the chin down and roll head slowly to the left side until the chin is over the shoulder. Now roll head back to the midline dipping the chin down and then up to the right shoulder. Move gently and slowly from side to side. Never crank the neck around in a circle. If you have a tight place, move your head in that spot back and forth several times with short movements. You can feel it release as you move your chin up further toward your shoulder in that direction. (Breaks up stress and tension held in neck and shoulders.)

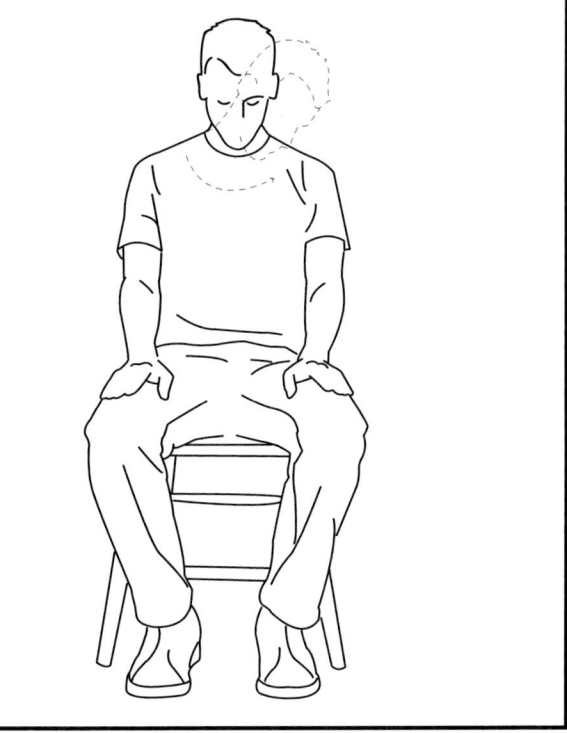

3.6.5 CHIN UP

Lower chin until it brushes the upper body. Slowly lift chin until it points upwards toward the ceiling; at that point clench the jaw and then release it. Lower chin again and repeat sequence 2X. Gently massage jaw joints on both sides of face and move jaw around a bit to release tension. (People hold tension in the jaw sometimes to the point of causing temporomandibular joint problems. The movements break up tension in the neck area and also in jaws.)

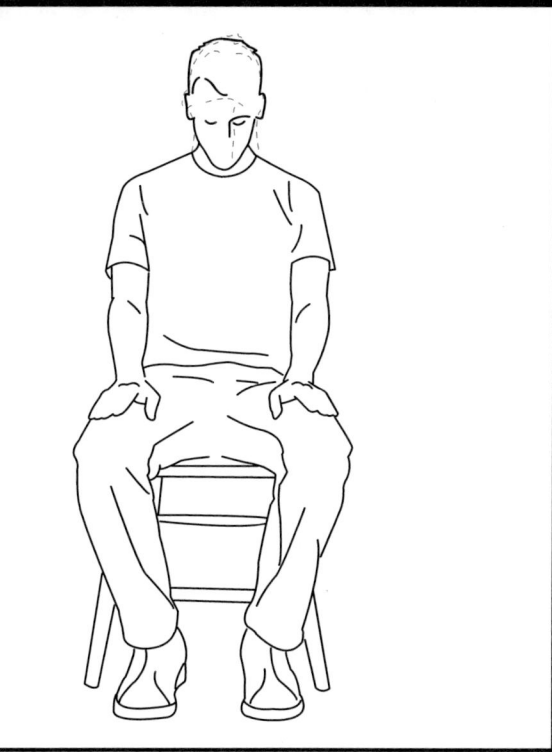

3.6.6 LOOKOUT NECK STRETCH

Place hand on opposite shoulder. Slowly turn head towards that shoulder until a gentle stretch is felt; hold 4 seconds. Keeping the hand in place, rotate head towards opposite shoulder giving a gentle stretch and hold 4 seconds. Bring head back to center and drop arm from shoulder. Next, put the other hand to opposite shoulder and repeat head turns. Repeat the entire sequence 2X. (Uses stretch to relax neck muscles.)

3.6.7 TRICEPS STRETCH

Bring the right hand back over the shoulder and reach down the spine with a gentle stretch to the count of 4. Relax and then do the same with the left hand. Repeat. (Uses stretch to relax muscles of arm, shoulder, and sides of body.)

3.6.8 CAT STRETCH

Extend both arms in front of the body. As if reaching for the opposite side of the room, perform a "cat stretch" by rolling the shoulders forward, straightening and stretching the arms and spreading fingers. Hold 4 seconds. Relax with arms resting back in the lap. Repeat 2X. (Stretches shoulder, elbow, and finger joints.)

3.6.9 APPLE PICKER

Reach overhead with one arm, looking up as you reach. Stretch up a little further as you extend fingers and open hand. As you lower that arm, start reaching up with the opposite hand and repeat the stretch. Repeat 2X. (Stretches shoulder, neck, elbow, and finger joints.)

3.6.10 ARM LENGTHENER

Extend one arm in front of body to 90 degrees as if reaching forward. The extended arm resists being moved or being pushed. Using the opposite open hand, the arm will be pressed just below the elbow in four directions to the count of four. Begin by pressing the arm downwards with an open hand; then curl the fingers to put pressure on the outer side of the arm by gently pulling towards midline. With an open hand press the arm on the inner side pressing away from midline. Lastly, press upward on the arm. Relax. Now reach both arms out in front and notice that the previously extended arm appears longer. Repeat motions using the opposite arm. Relax. Compare outstretched arms again. (Resistive exercises eventually result in muscle lengthening and relaxation.)

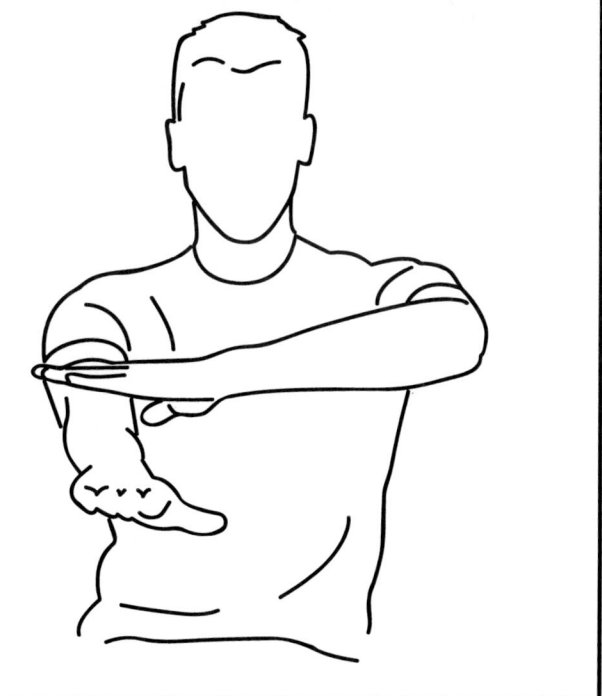

Copyright © 2005 Karen M. Moore

3.6.11 Wing It

Begin with arms at the side. Abduct arms to a 90-degree angle while flexing elbows and bringing fingertips to rest on the shoulder on the same side of body. Draw elbows together to meet at midline. Hold briefly to stretch. Relax and repeat. Next put hands behind head. Draw elbows to midline. Hold briefly to stretch. Relax and repeat. (Gives a great stretch to the shoulders and back.)

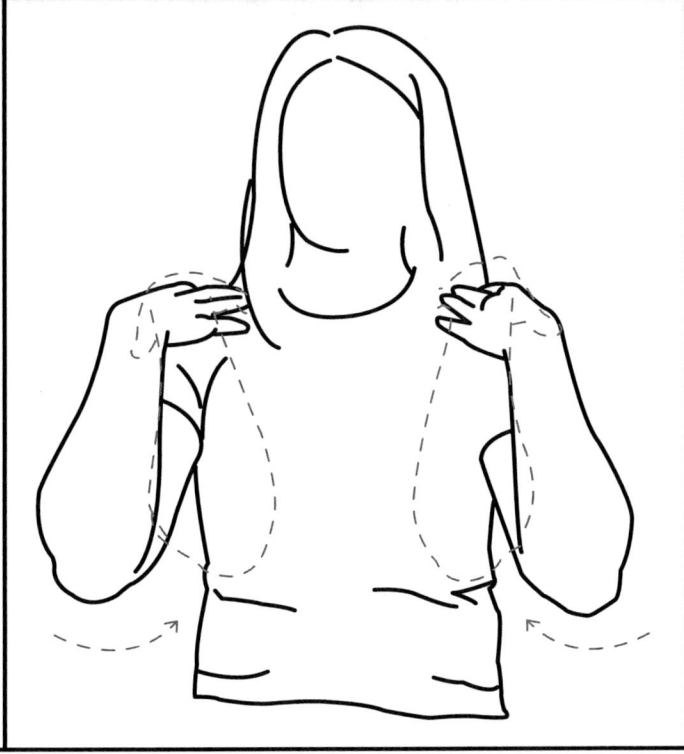

3.6.12 Cross Your Heart

Bend elbows and cross arms in front of body as hands are placed on opposite shoulders. Give a tight squeeze as if giving yourself a hug. Lower hands to the upper arm and squeeze again. Work down the arm squeezing at the elbows, forearm, and wrist.

Clasp hands firmly and then work back up arms in the reverse order ending with an extra firm squeeze to shoulders. Relax and uncross arms and note the feeling of the muscle release. (Provides deep pressure touch to the upper body.)

3.6.13 UPTIGHT PENGUIN

With arms at sides, shrug shoulders upward and hold for 4 seconds. Drop shoulders and stretch arms downward while tightening against body. Pretend to be pressing down with hands with wrists hyper extended and fingers open wide. Hold for 4 seconds. Relax and repeat. Next raise left shoulder up towards ear, hold briefly and drop back down. Repeat with right shoulder. Roll shoulders simultaneously 2X in a forward direction and then 2X in a backwards direction. (Breaks up tension in shoulder complex).

3.6.14 FENCE PAINTER

Extend one arm in front of body to 90 degrees. Wave arm and hand back and forth horizontally 4X (as if painting a fence) while extending and flexing wrist. Motion should be gentle and rhythmic. Repeat movements with opposite arm and hand. (Slow rhythmic movements are inhibiting or relaxing.)

Copyright © 2005 Karen M. Moore

3.6.15 HIGH HAND SHAKE

Flex arms to 90 degree in front of body. Bend elbows to 90-degree angle. Palms should face body. Move one hand towards shoulder on the same side of body while straightening the other arm at the elbow. Reverse and repeat gently and rhythmically 4X. (Uses rhythm to relax the body. Tests motor coordination and cerebellar function.)

3.6.16 HAND PRESS

Press palms together with fingers extended (as if in prayer) to the count of four. Release and gracefully drop hands to the sides of body. Repeat. Press palms together again and keeping gentle pressure, slowly move hands upwards and then downwards and then diagonally to one side and then the other. Finish by rotating pressed hands in a circle in front of body. Release and relax. (After experiencing contraction of muscles against resistance, it is easier to feel muscles relax and improves body awareness.)

3.6.17 FOOT FIXER

Point toes of one foot. Flex foot back and hold for a few seconds. Flexes should be strong enough to give a little stretch to the muscles and tendons in the back of the leg. Point again, flex again. Repeat 3X. Rotate foot at ankle. Notice if it is loose and easy to rotate. If not, repeat a few more foot flexes. Repeat motions with opposite foot. End by rotating both feet as if paddling feet in water. (Movements break up the tendon guard reflex which is activated in stress as body prepares for fight or flight. Try comparing looseness of ankle before and after this exercise.)

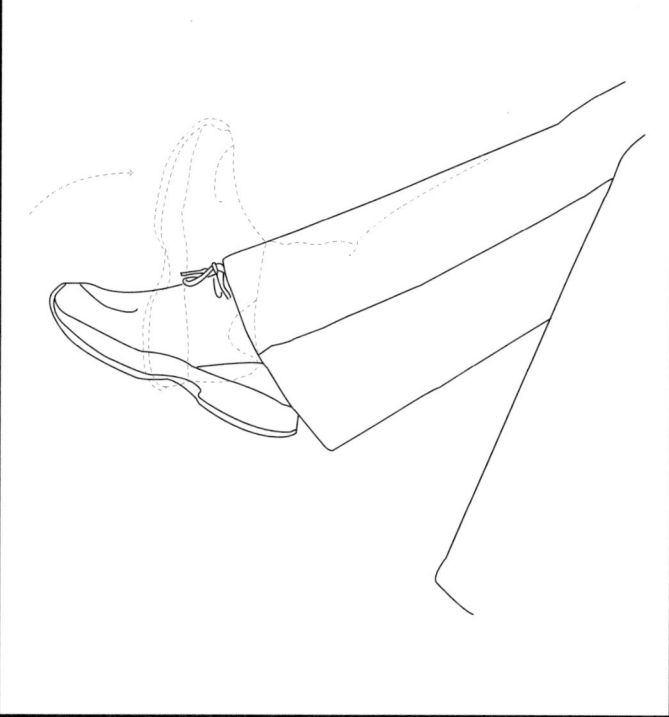

3.6.18 HEELS AND TOES

Rock feet back and forth. Start by rocking up on heels with foot flexed and then rock onto the toes lifting heels. Repeat 3X. (Gives stretch to heels feet and calf muscles; also works to relax tendon guard reflex.)

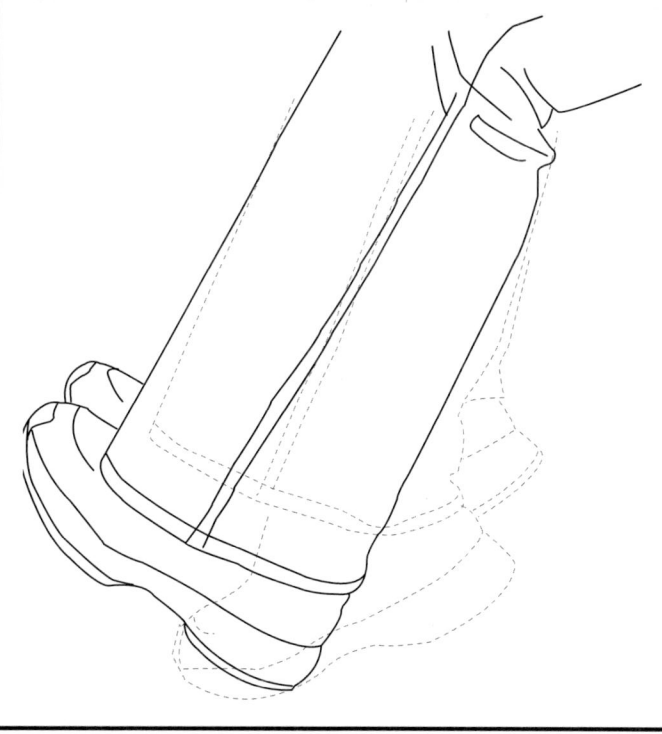

3.6.19 MARCHING IN PLACE

Place hands on thighs. Alternate lifting legs as if marching in place 6X (3 lifts for each leg). Repeat 2 more times. (Requires a shift in weight, forcing postural adjustment and practice with balance.)

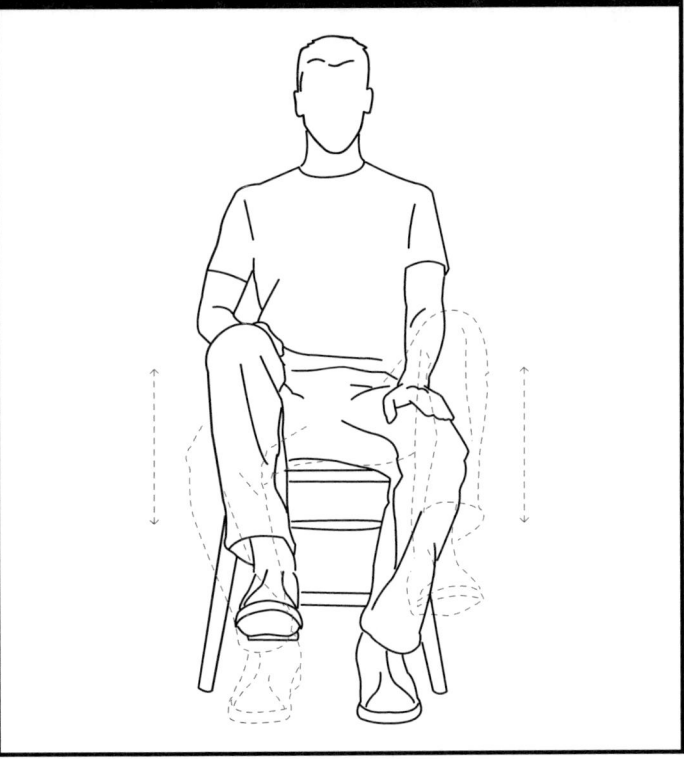

3.6.20 FOOT LEADER

Raise right leg until knee is fully extended; point toes and move leg back and forth horizontally 3X dipping slightly in the middle. Looks as if foot is conducting the band. Repeat with left leg and foot. (Gives stretch to knees, calves, thighs, and hip joint.)

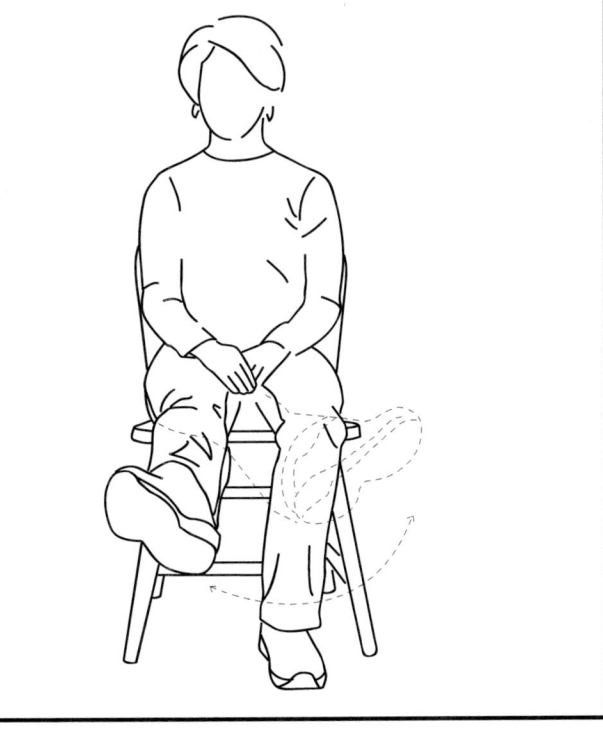

3.6.21 GLIDER / SLIDER

Extend arms to 90 degrees in front of body. Cross wrists and clasp hands, interlocking fingers. Cross ankles. Fold body forward and slide hands down legs towards ankles. Hold for 4 seconds. Do not force this stretch. Sit back up and then glide downwards again letting gravity produce a nice stretch of the back. Sit up again. Repeat gliding motions 2X. (Stretches and relaxes the back.)

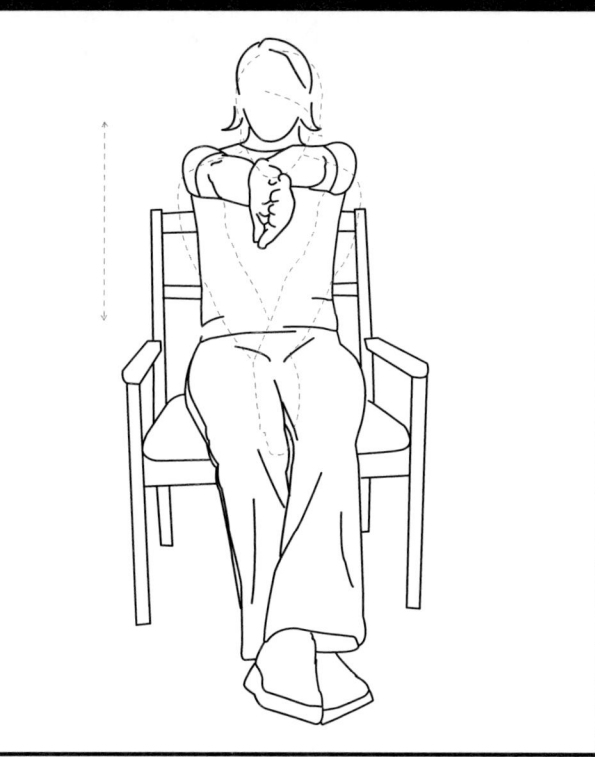

3.6.22 BEACH BALL CIRCLES

Hold arms out in front of body with hands approximately 30" apart and elbows slightly flexed. Pretend to be holding a large beach ball. Move hands and imaginary ball in a circular arch, first in one direction and then the other. Repeat 3X. (Rhythmic and relaxing. The circle is a cross-cultural symbol of unity and harmony.)

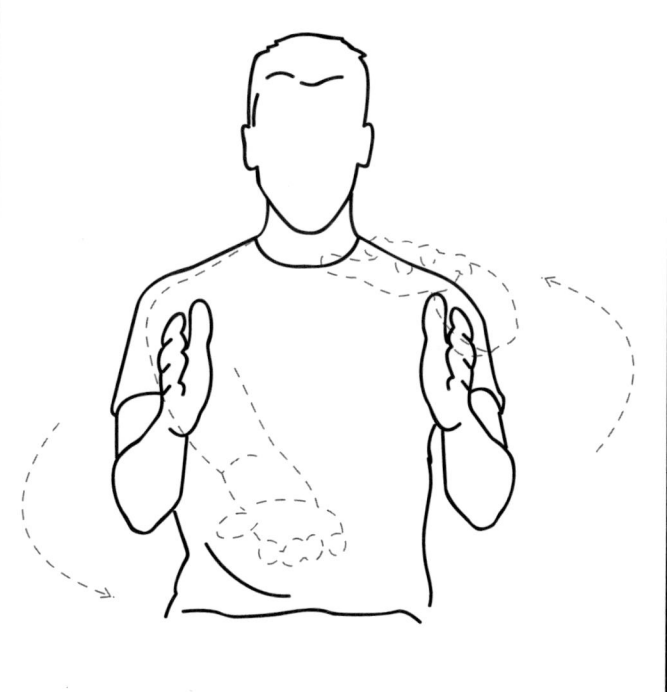

Copyright © 2005 Karen M. Moore

3.6.23 PEACOCK PECK

Flex elbows and hold hands in front of body about 20" apart with palms facing each other. Adduct fingers and curl to touch thumb forming an oval. Flex the wrist and drop the fingers downward and hold for 4 seconds for a gentle stretch. Open (abduct) fingers as wrist extends and then hyper extends. Hold for 4 seconds for a gentle stretch. Repeat 2X. (Provides range of motion and stretch to joints and wrists of hands. Helpful to patients with arthritis.)

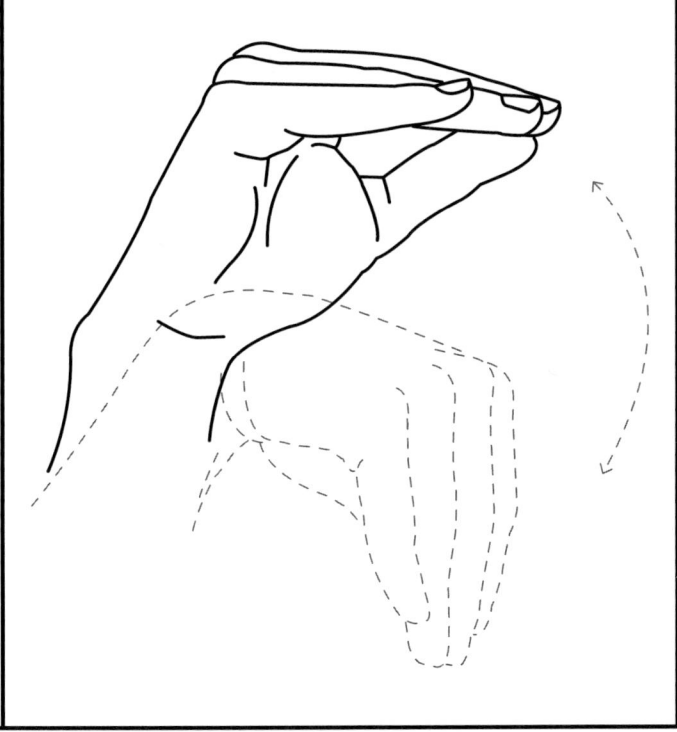

3.6.24 FINGER MANIPULATIONS

With both hands in front of body, palms facing, and elbows flexed, begin by rotating thumbs in one direction and then the other. Next, touch each finger to the thumb starting with index finger and ending with little finger. Reverse several times. Repeat starting with thumb rotations. End by pressing the tips of fingers of one hand against the matching fingertips of the other hand. Keep palms about 6" away from each other. Hold a slight pressure while slowly rotating hands away from body, back to center, and then towards the body and back to center. Repeat. (Provides sensory input to the multiple joints of the hand.)

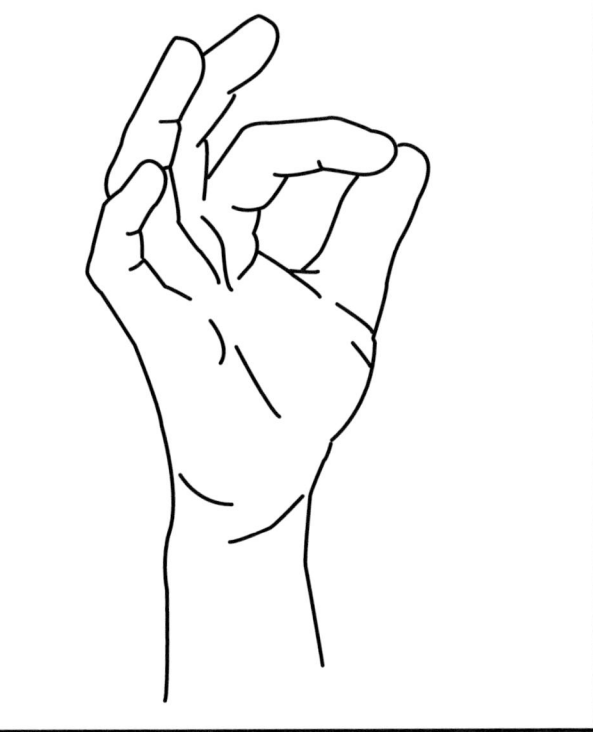

3.6.25 HAND MASSAGE

Begin by curling one hand into a loose fist. Wrap the other hand around it, and squeeze gently in short bursts while moving it around to give pressure to different areas. Now open first hand and massage palm and fingers with thumb of opposite hand. Give gentle traction to fingers by carefully pulling on them separately or together. Repeat with opposite hands. (Relaxes hands and helps to break up tension in the body. We wring our hands when we are upset to get the same response.)

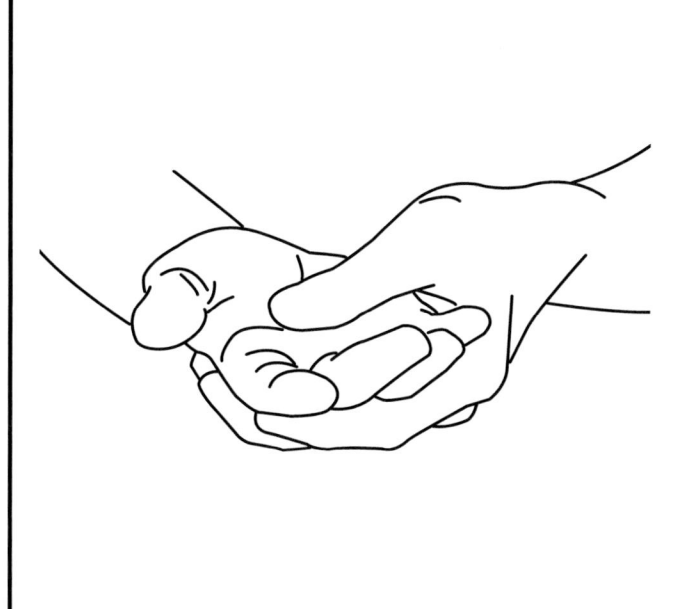

3.6.26 WAVE / SWIM

With one hand begin an exaggerated stroke-like wave motion. Start hand with wrist hyper-extended at about head level and stroke downward to waist level while gracefully flexing the wrist. As that hand approaches waist level begin wave with the opposite hand. Continue reversing hands in rhythmic dance-like wave motions for about 6 cycles. Next, turn the waves into an exaggerated swim stroke. While alternating arms extend elbows and reach forward and then pull back towards trunk as if swimming. Repeat for about 6 cycles. (Rhythm is relaxing. Sensory input is given to wrist, elbow and shoulder joints.)

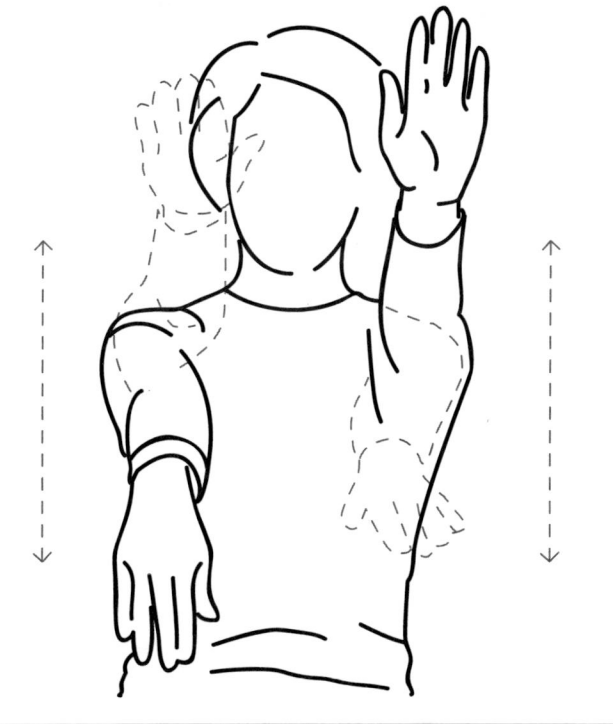

3.6.27 PALM UP / PALM DOWN

Begin with elbows flexed and both hands in front of body with palms turned downwards (pronation). Turn one palm up (supination) and then the other. Turn first palm down and then the second one down. Repeat in rhythmic alternating hand movements 6X. (Rhythmic, thus relaxing. Tests cerebellar function and ability to follow intricate movement pattern. This movement pattern can be made easier if hands are placed against thighs to provide additional tactile input.)

BREATHING ROUTINES

DIRECTIONS	The Standard Breathing Routine is performed midway through the Movement Routine. A way to help pace the breaths is to silently count to four as the deep breath is being drawn, as it is held, and then again as it is being released. Alternatives to this routine are as follows: ■ Use the Deep Breathing with A Sigh (instructions follow). ■ After completing the Standard Breathing Routine, encourage the patient to take three more breaths. ■ Repeat the Standard Breathing Routine. ■ Use the Standard Breathing Routine midway through the Movement Routine. At the end of the Movement Routine, conduct the Deep Breathing with a Sigh.

3.6.28 STANDARD DEEP BREATHING

Tell the patients that they will be doing some deep breathing. Say:

- **First, make sure you are doing abdominal breathing and not shallow breathing. Put your hand on your abdomen. You should feel it rise and fall as you breathe.**

- **Next, before you take that first deep breath, get rid of all the stale air in your lungs by puffing out the air with three strong puffs. Then we will take a nice deep breath through the nose.**

- **Let's all begin with the three puffs.** (Therapist demonstrates the audible puffs.)

- Now take that nice slow deep breath.

- **Hold it for a few seconds.** (Usually to the silent count of four).

- Now release the breath slowly, relaxing as you let the breath go.

- Now take in another deep breath.

- Hold it.

- Now let it out very slowly. Imagine all your tension going out with your breath.

- **Repeat with one or two more breaths.**

3.6.29 DEEP BREATHING WITH A SIGH

This breathing activity is done exactly like the previous one except, that on exhalation, the patient releases a long sigh with the breath. The sigh releases tension, especially in the pectoral muscle area.

Give the following directions:

- This time when we exhale our breath we are going to release it with a big sigh. This helps to break up tension. I want to hear an audible sigh. When you let out the sigh, I want you to imagine that you are melting into the chair as you relax.

- Now take that nice slow deep breath.

- **Hold it for a few seconds.** (Usually to the silent count of four.)

- Now release the breath slowly, sighing as you let the breath go.

- Now take in another deep breath.

- Now release the breath slowly with an audible sigh and imagine yourself melting into the chair.

Copyright © 2005 Karen M. Moore

Stage II: Examples of Two Movement Routines

To guide the leader in developing a Movement Routine, two possible routines follow. The number next to the exercise indicates its identification number in the Handout. Leaders can design their own routines by choosing 20 out of the 27 movements.

SUGGESTED MOVEMENT ROUTINE 1	SUGGESTED MOVEMENT ROUTINE 2
Start Up (3.6.1)	Start Up (3.6.1)
Rock + Roll (3.6.2)	Rock + Roll (3.6.2)
Look Out Neck Stretch (3.6.6)	Trunk Turns (3.6.3)
Cat Stretch (3.6.8)	Neck Rolls (3.6. 4)
Applepicker (3.6.9)	Chins Up (3.6.5)
Wing It (3.3.11)	Triceps Stretch (3.6.7)
Cross Your Heart (3.6.12)	Arm Lenghtener (3.6.10)
Uptight Penguin (3.6.13)	Cross Your Heart (3.6.12)
Fence Painter (3.6.14)	Fence Painter (3.6.14)
Hand Press (3.6.16)	High Hand Shake (3.6.15)
Standard Deep Breathing (3.6.28)	**Standard Deep Breathing (3.6.28)**
Foot Flexer (3.6.17)	Foot Flexer (3.6.17)
Glider/slider (3.6.21)	Heels And Toes (3.6.18)
Marching In Place (3.6.19)	Marching In Place (3.6.19)
Beach Ball Circles (3.6.22)	Foot Leader (3.6.20)
Peacock Peck (3.6.23)	Beach Ball Circles (3.6.22)
Finger Manipulations (3.6.24)	Peacock Peck (3.6.23)
Hand Massage (3.6.25)	Finger Manipulations (3.6.24)
Wave/swim (3.6.26)	Wave/swim (3.6.26)
Palm Up/palm Down (3.6.27)	Hand Press (3.6.16)
Breathing With A Sigh (3.6.29)	**"On Your Own" Deep Breathing**

ACTIVITY DIRECTIONS 3.7

SENSE-ABILITY GROUP
Stage III: The Conversing Stage

Time: 2 minutes

Patient Recognition and Comments

PATIENT REGOGNITION AND COMMENTS	
DIRECTIONS	After completing the Movement Routine, ask the patients to comment on their experience of the exercises. The questions are directed in such a way as to help patients understand the importance of the movements and deep breathing after discharge. Questions should vary from session to session or ask patients different questions during the same session. Example Questions ■ Were you able to relax with the exercises? ■ What was your favorite movement or activity? ■ Was there an area of the body that felt good to stretch? ■ Do you carry your tension in any particular place? Which exercises helped in that area? ■ How could you use helpful movements in your daily routine (e.g., foot flexes in the morning or before bed or in bed when sleep is difficult, stretches during brief breaks at work, shoulder shrugs or hugs when feeling tense)? ■ Did you enjoy the deep breathing? ■ When could you benefit from using the deep breathing techniques (e.g., times of stress, upon rising, breathing breaks interspersed throughout the day, at bedtime)?

Copyright © 2005 Karen M. Moore

SENSE-ABILITY GROUP
Stage IV: The Sensing Stage

Time: 4 minutes

Choose ONE ACTIVITY per session

3.8.1 ACTIVITY 1 BEANBAG TAPPING

MODALITY	Deep pressure touch
MATERIALS	One beanbag for each patient. Beanbags can be purchased or handmade and should fit easily in the palm of the hand. Beanbags can be made from heavy fabric such as denim or corduroy and filled with beans or seed corn from the feed store. Begin with two, four-inch squares of fabric, right sides together. Sew ½" from the edge around the square, leaving a small opening for stuffing. Turn, fill with beans, and sew opening.
DIRECTIONS	Have patients choose a beanbag. Ask patients to hold the beanbag with one hand and begin tapping firmly on the palm and back of the other hand. Then have them move up the arm. The shoulders are next, including the pectoral muscles in front. Repeat on the opposite side and now ask them to tap as much of the back as they can reach comfortably. Stop briefly and ask patients if they can feel the tingly effect of the tapping. Move on to tap the legs. Thighs, knees, shins, calves and feet are tapped. When everyone is finished tapping, throw the beanbags into a basket in the center of the group.
DISCUSSION	How does your body feel when you finish tapping? Do you hold your tension in any particular place such as the shoulders? Be sure to do some extra tapping on areas that hold tension.

3.8.2 ACTIVITY 2 MEDICINE BALL

MODALITIES	Proprioception, deep pressure touch
MATERIALS	One heavy vinyl or leather-covered Medicine Ball. Sizes vary, but the one we used was about the size of a basketball and weighed about nine pounds. Medicine balls are used during training in sports such as boxing.
DIRECTIONS	Have one patient begin performing simple exercises with the Medicine Ball. He should begin by slowly lifting the ball over his head, shifting the weight of the ball from hand to hand just above the lap, and rolling the ball down his outstretched legs as far as possible without letting go of the ball. Pass it to the next patient who repeats the exercise. Continue until all patients have had a turn.
DISCUSSION	How much do you think the ball weighs? What feels better: lifting the ball or rolling down the legs?

3.8.3 ACTIVITY 3 EXERCISE BAND ROWING

MODALITIES	Vestibular input, proprioception
MATERIALS	A 4-foot length of blue (extra heavy) exercise band with the ends knotted together in a firm knot. Theraband™ is one brand name for a 4" wide elastic product that provides graded resistance for strengthening activities; each color represents a different grade. Similar products are available and are called resistance bands or exercise bands.
DIRECTIONS	A ring of exercise band is used to create a two man rowing technique. Hold one end of the exercise band circle with two hands (volar surface of hand up, downward grasp), and have a patient holds the other side in the same manner. Begin by rocking back and pulling the exercise band towards you. Instruct the patient to "bend forward towards me, extend your arms. Now pull me." Reverse the motion. After a few more repetitions of instructions, "Bend forward again with me, pull me back," a rhythm is established and patients row back and forth approximately 10 to 15 more times.
DISCUSSION	What exercise or sport does this activity resemble (e.g., rowing machine, rowing a boat)?

3.8.4 ACTIVITY 4 PARACHUTE GAMES

MODALITIES	Proprioception, vestibular input, vision
MATERIALS	One, six or twelve foot diameter colorful nylon fabric parachute. Most have handles spaced around the edges to hold onto.
DIRECTIONS	Have patients seated and evenly distributed in a circle about the size of the parachute. Ask the patients to hold the edges of the parachute. Instruct them to raise the parachute quickly over their head so that all of the patients can be seen underneath. Do this several times as the patients try to coordinate their efforts. Put a ball in the center of the parachute to play a game and have patients try to bounce it up to the ceiling. "Popcorn" is another game; patients jounce one or two balls up and down in random fashion on the parachute. Another game is the "name game." Call out a name and the patients try to roll the ball over to that individual.
DISCUSSION	Has anyone ever used a real parachute? What sensations arise from this activity (e.g., feeling the muscles work, the swish sound of the parachute, feeling the breeze it creates)?

Copyright © 2005 Karen M. Moore

SENSE-ABILITY GROUP
Stage V: The Acting and Interacting Stage

Time: 16 minutes

Choose TWO ACTIVITIES per session (17 total activities)

3.9.1	ACTIVITY 1 INDOOR BOCCE
MATERIALS	Disc-O-Bocce. This is an indoor version of the popular game Bocce. The game consists of nine flat rubbery disks, one pink and four sets of other colors.
DIRECTIONS	The pink disk is used as the target, just as the small ball is used in outdoor Bocce. Place the pink disk in the center of the circle of players. The other disks are passed out, one to a patient. Players look about to find someone with the same disk color; that person will be their partner. Partners decide who will go first and who will wait for the second round. Suggest that the disks be thrown Frisbee style. Ask for a "volunteer" to throw the disk at the pink disk; the designated partner takes a turn until one of each color disk has been thrown. Sometimes the disks roll around if not thrown right; the player is allowed to try again. The remaining disks are thrown in turn for the second round. The pair of disks closest to the pink disk wins. Guide the patients in problem solving together to determine the average distance of the paired disks to find the closest pair, as opposed to just the closest disk.
DISCUSSION	This is our most popular game. One distinct advantage of this game is that many patients are involved congruently. It provides many social and problem solving opportunities.

3.9.2 ACTIVITY 2 THE NAME GAME

MATERIALS	One of any of the following items: Koosh ball (soft and fluffy ball that appears to be made from hundreds of elastics), a beanbag, a soft inflatable indoor Frisbee, a large therapy ball, or any soft interesting object.
DIRECTIONS	Begin by explaining the simple rules: ■ Say your name first and then the name of the person you want to throw the ball to. ■ If you don't know their name, just ask; that is why we are doing this activity. ■ I'll start, "My name is Karen and I'm throwing the ball to Mary." Have patients take turns throwing the ball to peers and staff. If a large therapy ball is used, ask the players to roll it to one another. After each person has had several turns, ask for a volunteer to try to name the other players. Some patients will be capable of naming everyone in the group, and they usually volunteer to do so. When they finish, prompt the remaining patients to try to name one or two people. Provide, when needed, generous praise. This game lasts about five to eight minutes.
DISCUSSION	Excellent game for newcomers or large groups. It is also a good assessment of memory.

3.9.3 ACTIVITY 3 BALLOON GAME

MATERIALS	A large heavy-duty balloon, 9" works well.
DIRECTIONS	The objective of the game is to keep the balloon from hitting the floor. Have one patient toss the balloon in the air and instruct patients to tap it from one person to another. They can tap it to the person next to them or across the room. The game ends when the balloon hits the floor. The balloon can also be used to play a volleyball type game. The net is imaginary. Have patients imitate various volleyball shots. No score is kept.
DISCUSSION	This game is very engaging and can be useful when a patient has been resisting participation. Patients probably laugh more during this game than in any other game. It has been noted that some patients with schizophrenia avoid this game, perhaps because of the unpredictability of the balloon.

Copyright © 2005 Karen M. Moore

3.9.4 ACTIVITY 4 FLOOR BASKETBALL

MATERIALS	A "floor Basketball hoop" made of PVC. These freestanding hoops are available through equipment catalogs. One version is actually designed for the pool, the "Pro Water Basketball Game." An 8" ball is used that is soft enough to be safe yet able to be bounced.
DIRECTIONS	Place the PVC hoop in front of you and demonstrate ways to toss the ball into the hoop such as overhand, underhand, one hand, two hands, one bounce in and so on. Then, put the hoop in front of the first patient at a distance that is slightly challenging. Explain that this person can choose a way to throw the ball into the hoop, and the rest of the group has to do it the same way. Patients all take one turn throwing the ball like the first player, then another person chooses a new way to toss the ball into the hoop, and another round is played.

Another way to play is that if a person misses the hoop, the next person chooses a new way of tossing the ball, and the patients continue taking turns until someone misses again and then another new way is chosen. Continue to adjust the challenge of the hoop placement for each person. A more success-oriented way to play is to adjust the hoop until the player is successful. |

3.9.5 ACTIVITY 5 INDOOR BASKETBALL

MATERIALS	A ring or indoor basketball hoop. A variety of Koosh balls makes the game more challenging.
DIRECTIONS	Give the first patient four Koosh balls. While standing, hold the hoop up in front of the patient at a distance deemed an appropriate challenge. Have the patient throw the balls into the hoop. If one misses the hoop, hand it back for another try. House rules say that you have to try until you get at least one ball into the hoop. Have patients take turns. Choose a player familiar with the game to hold the hoop. Give cues to hold the hoop at an appropriate distance for each person.
DISCUSSION	Because many patients have played basketball on teams or as a backyard sport, it brings up opportunities to discuss interests and leisure.

ACTIVITY DIRECTIONS (page 4 of 9) 3.9

3.9.6 ACTIVITY 6 VELCRO TARGET GAMES

MATERIALS	A large indoor dart game that has Velcro on the target and fuzzy balls that stick to the Velcro. One is called the Jumbo Dart Ball Game. The target is a 25" circular vinyl "pillow" covering an internal inflatable, which is light, compact and portable for traveling. Colorful Velcro patches provide targets, the center patch being worth 100 points, the middle piece being worth 50 points, and the outer circle being worth 25 points. Three fuzzy tennis type balls are used to throw as darts. There is a smaller version. Similar indoor target games are available.
DIRECTIONS	Hold the large target in front of each patient at an appropriate distance to make the activity challenging. Have the player aim the fuzzy balls at the target and calculate the score. Players take turns. In the second round, they try to beat their previous score. The emphasis is on personal achievement, not on competitiveness. Designate a patient who is familiar with the game to hold the target. The target can also be put on the floor or propped in a chair or hung from the blackboard.
DISCUSSION	Offers on opportunity to assess math skills as patients add up scores.

3.9.7 ACTIVITY 7 RUBBER TIPPED DARTS

MATERIALS	An indoor dart game. One is made by Pressman and called the "Round Striker." The three pink and three blue darts are rubber tipped.
DIRECTIONS	Hang the dartboard on a large blackboard, which deflects stray darts. Have the patient stand at a designated distance from the target marked by a beanbag on the floor. Divide the patients into two teams, the pink team and the blue team. This game is challenging and may require several practice shots and extra tries. One team member takes a turn throwing the three colored darts at the target. The score is calculated according to the color key on the board and can be written on the blackboard. A member of the other team takes a turn and that score is written on the blackboard. Team members take turns until everyone has played. The final score can be calculated to determine the winning team.
DISCUSSION	This game is not appropriate for manic or impulsive patients. It is challenging.

Copyright © 2005 Karen M. Moore

3.9 ACTIVITY DIRECTIONS (page 5 of 9)

3.9.8 ACTIVITY 8 REACHER TOSS

MATERIALS	A reacher, preferably one that has two tips that rest evenly on the floor. One brand is called E-Z Reacher. Another brand is called the "Golden Retriever." Also have a variety of items that can be picked up with a reacher; items ranging in size from a cedar block to a penny. Use a plastic shoebox to store the objects; it can also be used as the target.
DIRECTIONS	Place the items on the floor in front of the patient with the box put at a distance deemed reasonable for challenge and success. Have patients take turns using the reacher to pick up the items and then fling or drop them into the box, depending on their capability. Grade the game by changing the distance of the box or the size and shape of the items. A game variation is to use six of the same items, such as six soft stress balls. In this case, the target can be moved further away. The emphasis here is on the perceptual motor skills of tossing the items into the box and to see how many of the six balls reach the target.
DISCUSSION	This activity also provides a forum for education regarding adaptive equipment.

3.9.9 ACTIVITY 9 RING TOSS

MATERIALS	Indoor ring toss game. One traditional version consists of a wooden crossbar with 5 colored pegs, one in the center and four at the ends of the crosspieces. It comes with four flexible rubber rings. Another version consists of a colorful peg target and hemp rings.
DIRECTIONS	Place the target in front of a player at an appropriate distance for challenge and success. The player tosses the four rings onto the target. The rings can be given back to the player if she misses. The house rule is that a person needs to try until he or she gets one ring over the target. The traditional wooden game has point scores for each of the five pegs and a score can be totaled. In the second round, patients can try to beat their previous score.

3.9.10 ACTIVITY 10 HORSESHOES

MATERIALS	Indoor horseshoe set. They are readily available in catalogs and toy stores.
DIRECTIONS	The easiest way to play is to use one base, which is placed at an appropriate distance in front of each player. A few practice turns will probably be necessary. Have the players take turns throwing all four of the horseshoes onto the base. The game can also be played in a more traditional way by forming two teams and using two bases placed about 12' apart. One team member takes a turn throwing the horseshoes at the more distant target and then the opposite team member takes a turn. Keep score by giving two points for a full ringer and one point for a partial ringer or leaner. Have players' alternate turns until everyone has played.
DISCUSSION	This is a familiar and popular game that provides an opportunity to discuss leisure and sports activities.

3.9.11 ACTIVITY 11 THE BUCKET GAME

MATERIALS	Three heavy-duty buckets of different colors that have been weighted to prevent them from being knocked over (any flat heavy object can be duck taped to the inside bottom). Five Kooshes or interesting beanbags. Six file cards, each with three-color coded labels or stickers that match the colors of the buckets. The three dots are marked with the six variations possible for 5, 10, and 20 points (5-10-20, 5-20-10, 10-5-20, 10-20-5, 20-10-5, 20-5-10).
DIRECTIONS	Set the three buckets up in front of the first player. Show the person next to him the six cards and ask him to select one and not show the card to anyone else. This card will determine the number of points each bucket is worth. The player throws the Koosh Ball or beanbags into the buckets of choice. He can throw all of them in one bucket or distribute them. The person holding the selected file card reports the point value of the buckets, and the player and the leader total the score. For example, suppose the blue bucket is worth 5 points, the red one 10 points, and the yellow one 20 points. If the player threw 2 Kooshes in the blue bucket, 2 in the red, and one in the yellow the total score would be 50 points. Have players continue taking turns selecting a card for the points and tossing the Kooshes in the buckets.
DISCUSSION	Excellent game for assessing math skills and ability to follow the group process and take turns.

Copyright © 2005 Karen M. Moore

3.9 ACTIVITY DIRECTIONS

3.9.12   ACTIVITY 12   GAME CENTER BASKETBALL

MATERIALS	An indoor basketball game center. Play Hut makes a Game Center version that has a basketball hoop and drop holes for added points and a ball return feature. Balls are light and made of hard plastic. Other similar versions are available.
DIRECTIONS	Place the basketball game in front of the seated patient. Give him four balls to shoot. A basket earns 10 points and the holes that the balls drop into are added points. Have patients take turns shooting baskets and tallying their score. In the second round, they try to beat their previous score.
DISCUSSION	Game is bright and colorful and captures interest. It is easily gradable to add challenge for capable patients.

3.9.13   ACTIVITY 13   INDOOR GOLF

MATERIALS	One-hole auto return putting carpet 1 foot wide by 9 feet long. Dense foam golf balls. A golf club designed for indoor use, 32-35 inches long. Other similar designs are available.
DIRECTIONS	Demonstrate putting safely from a designated spot on the carpet. Have patients take turns putting the balls up the carpet and toward the hole. This may require several tries. Grade the game by placing the ball nearer to the hole.
DISCUSSION	Because many patients have played golf or miniature golf in the past, this game taps leisure interests. It is very challenging and somewhat hard to grade difficulty.

3.9.14   ACTIVITY 14   DICE AND HOOPS

MATERIALS	Two large 6" vinyl coated dice. Two hoops, approximately 22" in diameter.
DIRECTIONS	Set two hoops in front of the patient. They should overlap by 10 inches. Have the patient toss or roll the two large dice into the rings. A score is determined by the number of dots on the upturned side of any die in or touching the outer rings. The score of any die within or touching the overlap area is doubled. Total the score with the patient. Have patients take turns; on the second round they try to beat their previous scores.
DISCUSSION	This game offers assessment opportunities to assess math skills and problem solving.

3.9.15 ACTIVITY 15 KOOSH WOOSH FRISBEE RINGS AND CONES

MATERIALS	Four lightweight flat Koosh Woosh Frisbee rings: two large and two small. Four 12" plastic cones. Spectrum makes another version of rings; many variations are available.
DIRECTIONS	The four cones are set up in front of the patient in the form of a square, two in front and two in back. The patient attempts to fling the rings onto the cones. The large rings are worth one point each and the small rings are worth two points. The score is doubled if the rings land on the further cones. The patient and the leader tally the score. Players take turns. If a second round is played, the patient tries to beat their previous score.
DISCUSSION	This game allows opportunities for decision making and risk taking; patients decide whether to aim for the close cones or the more challenging distant ones.

3.9.16 ACTIVITY 16 DICE AND THERAPY BALL

MATERIALS	One, large foam die and a large therapy ball (exercise ball). Bright poster with the following directions printed on it made durable by covering it with clear contact paper.
DIRECTIONS	Have patients take turns rolling the die and then following the directions for the corresponding number: 1. Lift the ball over your head 2. Roll the ball back and forth 3X to the person opposite you. 3. Pass the ball around the circle of players starting on the left. 4. Pass the ball around the circle of players starting on your right. 5. Bounce the ball in front of you 5X. 6. Free pass
DISCUSSION	This is a good activity for reinforcing and assessing cognitive skills and problem solving.

Copyright © 2005 Karen M. Moore

3.9.17 ACTIVITY 17 INDOOR SHUFFLEBOARD

MATERIALS	Indoor shuffleboard set that includes a flat court mat, four cues, and eight disks. A shuffle toss game is also available and is scored similarly.
DIRECTIONS	Divide the patients into 2 teams and have two players, one from each team, stand at the ends of the mat. Each of them takes a turn sliding a disk towards the triangular scoreboard at the opposite end of the mat. Then the next two players, one from each team stand at the mat and slide a disk towards the triangular scoreboard. This is repeated with players of each team. The only team that scores is the one with the leading disk. If a disk of the winning team is behind the leading disk of the opponent, it is not scored. Another way to play is to add up the scores for all of the disks, regardless of which team is ahead. When disks touch the line or are partially in the square of a higher number, that higher score is given. Players can take extra turns if their disks do not stay on the mat. The players at the other end of the mat take turns. The game continues until all players have had a turn. The team with the highest score at that time wins.
DISCUSSION	This game provides opportunities for teamwork and encourages problem solving.

ACTIVITY DIRECTIONS 3.10.1

SENSE-ABILITY GROUP
Stage VI: The Learning Stage

Time: 18 minutes

Choose ONE ACTIVITY (total of 14 activities)

3.10.1	ACTIVITY 1 GESTURES
DESCRIPTION	Charade type game in which patients act out universal gestures such as "go away" or activity words such as playing volleyball or typing.
OBJECTIVE	To increase verbal and non-verbal self-expression. To improve ability to read the expressions of others. To improve concept formation and problem solving. To improve leisure awareness.
MATERIALS	Four sets of 3x5 cards. Each set (see below) should be a different color or have a symbol on the back to identify the set. Words to be acted out are printed on the opposite side. Suggestions for the words in each set follow. **Set 1: Universal gestures:** come here, stop, I'm choking, quiet, telephone for you, go away, help, good job (thumbs up), I don't know, it's hot, it's cold, just a little, can't hear you, tastes bad (yuck), tastes good (yummy). **Set 2: Gross Motor:** roller skating, batting a ball, jumping rope, jack-hammering, square dancing, golfing, paddling a canoe, riding a bike, rowing a boat, driving a car, cross country skiing, playing tennis, pushing a wheel barrow, picking apples, playing pool, sawing down a tree, petting a dog, reading a book, playing volleyball, playing ping pong. **Set 3: Fine Motor:** drinking tea, eating spaghetti, playing the piano, peeling an orange, painting a picture, trimming fingernails, signing your name, cutting up an onion, watering a plant, typing, playing video game, playing chess, reading, playing a clarinet, kneading dough, making pizza, knitting, playing cards. **Set 4: Opposites:** short/tall, hot/cold, love/hate, soft/hard, strong/weak, happy/sad, over/under, light/dark, laugh/cry, silly/serious, mean/kind, easy/difficult.
DIRECTIONS	Explain the need for non-verbal communication and that most words in this activity are familiar and easy to act out. Begin with Set 1: Universal Gestures, as they are the easiest. Pass out cards to patients. Have players act out the words or activity on the card, and the other patients try to guess the word. If a person is having difficulty with a card, suggest they pick another. There may be time for several sets of cards. Discuss each of the gesture activities.

Copyright © 2005 Karen M. Moore

3.10.2 ACTIVITY DIRECTIONS

3.10.2 ACTIVITY 2 GOALSETTING GAME

DESCRIPTION	Through the use of suggestion cards, patients identify possible goals that will help them stay healthy after discharge.
OBJECTIVE	To identify lifestyle changes and choices that will support mental and physical health and to foster problem solving and communication skills.
MATERIALS	30 brightly colored file cards with suggestions for health maintenance post discharge. Examples include: STAY SOBER GET OUT MORE CHECK OUT LIBRARY PROGRAMS ATTEND AA ATTEND DAY PROGRAM SHOWER DAILY IMPROVE A RELATIONSHIP VOLUNTEER SAY "NO" MORE OFTEN GO TO CLUBHOUSE START SWIMMING JOIN YMCA OR YWCA REACH OUT FOR HELP TAKE MEDS AS PRESCRIBED USE A PILLBOX & MED ROUTINE START A NEW LEISURE ACTIVITY GET HELP FOR BUDGETING & FINANCES ATTEND CHURCH TAKE A COURSE OR CRAFT LESSONS START JOGGING WALK DAILY JOIN A GYM NO DAYTIME NAPPING START USING A POCKET CALENDAR MEET FRIEND FOR COFFEE EVERY WEEK SPEND MORE TIME WITH FAMILY OR FRIENDS SEARCH FOR A JOB STOP SMOKING GO ON A SENSIBLE DIET START EXERCISE ROUTINE
DIRECTIONS	Distribute three cards randomly to each patient. Have each patient review the suggestions to see if one or more of the ideas are appropriate personal goals for him. If the choices seem inappropriate, the patient trades the cards for three more. Patients take turns discussing their chosen goals. Give feedback and ask patients to comment regarding the appropriateness of the goals and how they could they be implemented.

3.10.3 ACTIVITY 3 SAFETY AND LESIURE WORDS

DESCRIPTION	This is a "hangman" type game in which patients take turns at the blackboard choosing words and marking lines for each letter of the word or phrase; other players try to guess what it is. Players are given choices of words in the categories of safety or leisure.
OBJECTIVE	To assess and improve safety and leisure awareness, to foster attention and problem solving, to encourage playfulness and socialization, to offer leadership opportunities.

MATERIALS	10, 5"X7" cue cards with the category printed on the back. On front of the card a hint is printed in red at the top with three or four word choices printed in black underneath. Examples for both categories are listed below.
	
	Category: Safety
	
	1. *Hint* - Items found in a medicine cabinet.
	   Words - gauze pads, antibiotic cream, eye drops, adhesive tape
	
	2. *Hint* - Bathroom safety.
	   Words - rubber backed rug, grab bars, ground fault plugs, bath mat
	
	3. *Hint* - Kitchen safety.
	   Words - pot holders, fire extinguisher, cabinet locks, appliances with automatic shut offs
	
	4. *Hint* - Driving safety.
	   Words - seat belts, sun glasses, cup holders, air bags
	
	5. *Hint* - Traveling safety.
	   Words - sun screen, telephone numbers, medication organizer, first aid kit
	
	6. *Hint* - Storage safety.
	   Words - strong shelving, metal cabinets, absence of clutter, critter control
	
	7. *Hint* - Health maintenance.
	   Words - balanced meals, aerobic exercise, medication organizer, calendar for appointments, emergency numbers posted
	
	8. *Hint* – Hygiene.
	   Words - frequent showering, regular tooth brushing, clean clothing, shampoo and condition
	
	9. *Hint* - Walking safety.
	   Words - scan both ways, use crosswalks, obey signals, buddy system, comfortable shoes

3.10.3 ACTIVITY 3   SAFETY AND LESIURE WORDS *(CONTINUED)*

MATERIALS *(Continued)*	***Category: Leisure***
	
	1. *Hint* - Items to take camping.
	   Words - propane stove, lantern, sleeping bag, folding tent, bug repellant
	
	2. *Hint* - Items to take to the beach.
	   Words - liquids for thirst, sun block, blanket, cooler, snorkeling gear, beach ball, volleyball set
	
	3. *Hint* - Items to take to the movies.
	   Words - money, snacks, glasses, tissues
	
	4. *Hint* - Items to take on a picnic.
	   Words - basket or cooler, large blanket, bug spray, foods that don't spoil
	
	5. *Hint* - Board games.
	   Words - Monopoly, Clue, Sorry, Checkers, Backgammon
	
	6. *Hint* - Outdoor games.
	   Words - badminton, volleyball, catch, Frisbee, softball
	
	7. *Hint* - Outdoor activities.
	   Words - riding a bike, skiing, roller blading, hiking
	
	8. *Hint* - Outdoor activities.
	   Words - gardening, bird watching, walking the dog, sunbathing
	
	9. *Hint* - Social activities.
	   Words - square dancing, barbecue, meet for coffee, dinner party, pool party
	
	10. *Hint* – Games.
	    Words - ping pong, pool, tennis, racquetball, bocce, horseshoes

DIRECTIONS	Select a cue card, identify the category (safety or leisure) and give the card to a patient. Have the patient go to the blackboard and make short horizontal lines appropriate for the number of letters in the word (s). The patient gives the hint and the other patients take turns guessing the letter of the word. Letters that are part of the word are placed on the appropriate line; letters that are not part of the word are written at the top of the board. Those players guessing the correct letters have an opportunity to guess the word (this is a good time to prompt discussion). If a player guesses correctly, he or she becomes the next game leader.

3.10.4 ACTIVITY 4 WHO WOULD YOU CALL?

DESCRIPTION	Players take turns answering question cards that ask who they would call in a variety of situations. They also role-play what they would say when they made the call.
OBJECTIVE	To practice problem solving, to review safety strategies, to role-play responses in emergencies, to prepare for community re-entry.
MATERIALS	25+ brightly colored cards with the following questions printed on each one, beginning with the words: **Who would you call and what would you say:** If you took your meds twice by mistake? If you would like to stop drinking or drugging? If your symptoms come back? If you need a ride to the doctor? If your meds are not working? If you are tempted to drink? If you feel out of control and you think you might hurt someone? If you are suicidal? If you are lonely? If you have overdosed? If someone has harmed you? If you run out of meds? If you would like to do some volunteer work? If your doctor is on vacation? If you are having side effects? If you are having chest pain? If you would like to take art or craft lessons? If you think someone is trying to break into your apartment? If you have a cold but it is getting much worse? If you feel like hurting yourself? If you would like to take a course? If you would like some job training? If you are looking for something to do with your time? If you are interested in a clubhouse program? If you are upset and you just want to talk to someone?
DIRECTIONS	Have each patient select two cards. The patients take turns answering the questions on the cards. Ask them to role-play out what they would say to the person who answers the phone. Ask group members for additional suggestions and to share if they have ever encountered such a situation.

Copyright © 2005 Karen M. Moore

3.10.5 ACTIVITY 5 EMOTION GAMES

DESCRIPTION	Games are played with cards that have emotions depicted on them either in words or pictures. Patients act out the emotions or describe the feelings.
OBJECTIVE	To identify emotions; to increase self-expression of emotions; to learn self-regulation strategies in dealing with feelings.
MATERIALS	Flippers which flip in a tiddly-wink type fashion when pressed, small Kooshes, and 3x5 cards with an emotion printed on each card. Emotions can include: love, happiness, helplessness, anger, contentment, hate, puzzlement, caring, confidence, peacefulness, worry, panic, embarrassment, loneliness, apathy, excitement, feeling safe, fearfulness, numbness, frustration, nervousness, hopefulness, sadness, and silliness. (Note: Pre-made emotions cards and poster can be purchased through Therapro; see resource list in the Appendix of the Manual.)
DIRECTIONS TO GAME 1	Pass one emotion card to each patient. Have them take turns acting out the emotions. For reference, place a poster on the floor in the center of the group circle with various emotions printed on it.
DIRECTIONS TO GAME 2	Play the game on a table using a Flipper or play it on the floor using a Koosh or small beanbag. Spread the cards out in a random fashion. Have patients take turns flipping or tossing the Flipper or ball onto one of the emotions. The player must then answer questions about that emotion such as: Is this an emotion that you feel often? When was the last time you felt this way? How do you deal with the feeling? If the emotion is good, what is the one thing you could do to feel that way? If the emotion is bad, what is one thing you could do to avoid feeling that way?

3.10.6 ACTIVITY 6 SUPPORTS GAME

DESCRIPTION	Patients identify three supports that they utilize to support them when they are not feeling well by tossing beanbags onto appropriate squares labeled on a poster.
OBJECTIVE	To assess and facilitate coping skills; to identify community supports; to foster communication skills; to share ideas on community resources
MATERIALS	Three small Kooshes or three small beanbags. A foldable game board made from two foam boards that are taped together. The board is divided into twelve squares. Supports that are locally available are printed in each square. To keep the board and the game relatively simple, similar or related supports are grouped together in one square. Supports for patients can include: 1. Church & spirituality. 2. Case manager. 3. Support groups. 4. EMH (Emergency Mental Health). 5. Supported housing & Residence staff. 6. Clubhouses 7. AA, NA, Dual Diagnosis. 8. Day treatment & work re-entry programs. 9. VNA, Home health services. 10. Doctors, therapists. 11. Family, friends. 12. Outreach Programs- Project Hope, Warm Line.
DIRECTIONS	Place the support game board in the center of the group. Explain the game, pointing out and explaining any of the support options that may not be familiar to group members. Give the first patient three small Koosh balls or three small beanbags. This patient (or group leader) is very familiar with the game, and will serve as a role model. The patients throw the beanbags onto the squares that delineate their main supports. If they miss the square, they retrieve the beanbag and try again. Once the supports are selected, follow up with a few questions, such as: Which support would you use in an emergency? You chose the Clubhouse; could you explain this program to others? Do you feel that you have enough support? Are any of these supports new for you? Are there any supports mentioned on the board that you are thinking of trying? Do you have a support that is not referred to on the board?

Copyright © 2005 Karen M. Moore

3.10.7 ACTIVITY 7 SPORTS MATCHING GAME

DESCRIPTION	In this matching game, patients try to find pairs of various sports activities. Because the matching aspect is non-verbal, this game is a good choice for nonverbal or non-English speaking patients.
OBJECTIVE	To explore leisure interests, to improve concentration, memory and problem solving, to enhance social interaction such as turn taking, respect for others, to support peers and to foster self-esteem through success oriented activity.
MATERIALS	30 cards consisting of 15 duplicate pairs of pictures representing different sport activities. Pictures can be taken from sports stickers, equipment catalogs, and magazines. Duplicate catalogs with exact makes matching cards easier. Sports can include: basketball, baseball, tennis, volleyball, Frisbee, weight-lifting, hiking, biking, badminton, ping pong, soccer, swimming, roller blading, skiing, and sailing.
DIRECTIONS	Shuffle the cards and lay them out face up in columns on a low table in the middle of the group. Patients take turns trying to make matches. When a match is made, ask the patient about his experience or interest in the sports activity (e.g., have you ever done this activity, is there an expense involved, what equipment is needed, would you consider trying it). Invite group members to make comments as well. In the interest of giving everyone more opportunities to make matches, second turns are not usually given to those patients who do make a match. The game continues until all the pairs are matched up. The number of paired cards determines the length and difficulty of the game. The fewer the pairs, the easier the game becomes.

ALTERNATIVE VERSION PICTURE MATCHING GAME

DESCRIPTION	In this matching game, patients try to find pairs of various pictures.
MATERIALS	40 cards consisting of 20 duplicate pairs of pictures representing various subjects and activities. Duplicate catalogs with exact pictures make matching easier. Pictures can include leisure activities such as gardening, pictures of animals, humorous pictures, pictures of food items. The possibilities are endless, but simple and clear pictures work best.
DIRECTIONS	This game is played liked the Sports Matching Game. The objectives are the same. Focus questions on the patient's connection or experience with the particular pictures (e.g., have you ever owned one of these, have you ever done a similar activity, do you like these, does this strike your sense of humor).

ACTIVITY DIRECTIONS 3.10.8

3.10.8 ACTIVITY 8 RIDDLES

DESCRIPTION	Patients take turns asking each other riddles that are written on game cards.
OBJECTIVE	To experience humor; to promote and assess thinking skills and problem solving; to improve socialization.
MATERIALS	A set of 20+ riddles written on index file cards. The riddle should appear at the top of the card. The solution should appear upside down at the bottom of the card. The following traditional riddles work well because they have clear hints within them or else they involve play on words. ■ What has four wheels and flies? (A garbage truck) ■ How are an old car and a baby alike? (They both have a rattle) ■ Where does a sheep go for a haircut? (To the Baaa-Baaa Shop) ■ How is a party like a tennis game? (There is always a racket) ■ How are dogcatchers paid? (By the pound) ■ What do you get when you cross an owl and a goat? (A hootenanny) ■ When does it rain money? (When there is a change in the weather) ■ What is the difference between an old penny and a new nickel? (Four cents) ■ What is the scariest cheese? (Munster) ■ What could you call a sleeping bull? (A bulldozer) ■ What happens to ducks when you tell them too many jokes? (They quack up) ■ What room is never lived in? (A mushroom) ■ What has many teeth but never has cavities? (A comb) ■ What do you get when you cross an insect with a rabbit? (Bugs Bunny) ■ How do you stop a bull from charging? (Take away his credit card) ■ What do you call a cross between a lemon and a cat? (A sour puss) ■ Why must a doctor keep his temper? (He can't afford to lose his patients) ■ What is the tallest building in every city? (The library, it has the most stories) ■ What do you call a car you drive in the fall? (An autumn-mobile)
DIRECTIONS	Pass out riddle cards. Have players take turns asking the riddle on their card. Offer hints to help with connections between the question and answer. Patients enjoy being the jokester and the fact that they are the ones with the answer to the joke.

Copyright © 2005 Karen M. Moore

3.10.9 ACTIVITY DIRECTIONS

3.10.9 ACTIVITY 9 "GETTING TO KNOW YOU" GAME

DESCRIPTION	Patients learn about each other by answering questions about their likes, dislikes, and opinions on various subjects.
OBJECTIVE	To encourage self-esteem and socialization, and to improve self-expression.
MATERIALS	25+ brightly colored file cards with the following questions printed on them: Name a characteristic you like in others. Tell about a pet in your life. Name someone who has been a good support to you over the years. Name one thing you like about yourself. What cartoon is your favorite? Why? Name someone you look up to. Have you ever had a nickname? What is it? With whom are you comfortable sharing your feelings? What is something about yourself that you are working to improve? What character from T.V. or the movies are you most like? Tell about a time when you helped someone. Name someone you wish you had a better relationship with. If you could change one thing about the world, what would it be? Describe one of your strengths. If you could take a trip anywhere in the world, where would you go? Tell about a time when someone helped you out. What would your closest friend say he or she likes about you? Name one healthy thing that you do for leisure. Name something that you think is beautiful. Compliment the person to your left. Name something you don't like to do, but you do it anyway. What person is your biggest support? Describe an accomplishment in your life. Describe a former hobby that you that you would like to get back into. If you were given $100 to spend on yourself, how would you spend it?
DIRECTIONS	Give patients two game cards. Ask them to begin by answering one of the questions about themselves. In the second round, ask them to read the question on the second card and ask someone else in the group to answer it. Continue with more questions if time allows.

3.10.10 ACTIVITY 10 MUSIC ACTIVITIES

DESCRIPTION	Patients listen or dance or sing to popular music and the oldies.
OBJECTIVE	To recall former interests; to reconnect with the experience and joy of music and dancing; to role model enjoyment; to foster social interaction; to assess memory, balance and motor skills.
MATERIALS	Create tapes or CDs by copying appropriate music from a variety of other tapes or CDs. Words for sing-a-long tunes can be typed. A tape can be made of one-minute sound bites for "Name That Tune." Tapes and CDs that can be purchased that have worked well for us include: Music For All Occasions (1991 K-Tel International Inc.) Party Music (1994 Turn Up The Music, Inc.) Rock Around The Oldies, Volume 3 (MCA Special Products MCAC 20529) All-Time Favorite Dances (Kimbo, Box 447, Long Branch, NJ, 07740) 1962 Billboard-Top Rock'n Roll Hits (1993 Rhino Records, Inc., 1035 Santa Monica Blvd., Los Angeles, CA. 90025) (note: All Billboard tapes are excellent) Forrest Gump: The Soundtrack (1994, Sony Music Entertainment, Inc. New York, N.Y. 10022)
DIRECTIONS	Tapes or CDs are used in a variety of ways. Sing-alongs: Distribute copies of words to familiar songs. Patients sing along. Dancing: Play dance songs. Encourage patients to try the dance, usually with a leader. If the dance songs are long, use only part of the tune. Fast-forward the tape to popular songs. Ask patients to recall the group famous for a song, the setting that the song or dance is associated with, the decade in which the title was popular, and so on. Name That Tune: Fast forward through a collection of popular songs, stopping at select songs. Ask patients to identify song titles, groups, eras, etc. Use the songs as conversation starters.

Copyright © 2005 Karen M. Moore

3.10.11 ACTIVITY 11 ASSERTIVENESS GAME

DESCRIPTION	Patients practice assertive responses to sample situations.
OBJECTIVE	To develop assertiveness, to improve problem solving, and to improve self-expression.
MATERIALS	30+ brightly colored file cards with the following questions printed on each one, beginning with the words *What could you say if:* Someone asks for your last cigarette? Someone asks to keep your lighter or matches rather than turning them in at the desk? Someone is pestering you for drugs? Someone is discouraging you from taking your medications? Someone has been pestering you for money? The tenants upstairs have been playing loud music at night and disturbing your sleep? Your electric bill appears to be wrong? Someone says something mean to you about your illness? You are trying to stay sober and a friend wants you to go to a bar? A relative is constantly asking for rides and never helps pay for gas? Your siblings do not understand that you can no longer care for your sick mother? Your watch is missing and your roommate appears to be wearing it? You don't understand why the doctor has you taking a new medication? You know you are starting to get very ill again? Who would you reach out to? You have been waiting in a long line and someone cuts in front of you? You don't remember what your doctor told you about a new medication? Your roommate is always leaving dirty clothes and dishes for you to pick up? Your partner does not understand your illness and expects you to "snap out of it"? Your roommates are engaged in a loud argument, and it is making you nervous? You are angry at your best friend because they never seem to make time for you? Your friend is always borrowing things and never returns them? You are uncomfortable because your roommate invites strangers to your apartment? Someone is pestering you for a date, and you do not want to go out with the person? A sales person comes to your door, and you are not interested in the product? Your boss is putting unreasonable expectations on you? Your friend wants to go to a restaurant that you feel is too expensive? Your roommate hasn't been showering, and it is getting offensive? You are not feeling well yet your son is pestering you to baby-sit for the grandchildren?
DIRECTIONS	Begin by reviewing the characteristics of passive, assertive, and aggressive communication styles. Place the cards face down on the floor or table. Have patients take turns tossing a Koosh on one of the cards. The patient then asks the person next to him the question on the card. If needed, read the identified card for the patient. Have the patient respond in an assertive manner to the question. Ask other group members to give suggestions.

3.10.12 ACTIVITY 12 DISCHARGE PLANNING GAME

DESCRIPTION	Patients take turns rolling a large die and answering questions that support health after discharge.
OBJECTIVE	To promote problem solving, coping skills, and healthy decisions regarding discharge plans.
MATERIALS	One large, 6" rubber die. A large hoop. A brightly colored poster with the following 6 discharge planning questions printed on it in large letters. The poster can be covered with clear Contact™ paper for durability.
DISCHARGE PLANNING QUESTIONS	1. Describe something you are going to do differently after discharge in order to stay healthy. 2. How could you improve a relationship when you leave? 3. Who is your biggest support? Can you ask for their help if needed? 4. What is one thing that worries you about being discharged? 5. Name a new support that you are adding following discharge. 6. How are you going to keep busy and active when you leave?
DIRECTIONS	Set up the poster with the Discharge Planning Questions so all can read it. Have patients take turns rolling the die into the hoop and answering the question on the poster that corresponds to the number on the die. When a number appears again, the patient has to give a different answer or idea. Continue taking turns until everyone has had a chance to answer a question. A second or third round can be played if the group is small and time allows.

ALTERNATIVE VERSION DISCHARGE PLANNING GAME

MATERIALS	Questions are mounted on separate cards with 1 – 6 large dots on the back to match the dots on the die.
DIRECTIONS	Distribute the question cards to patients. Have them take turns rolling the die into the hoop; the patient holding the card corresponding to the number of dots on the die reads the question. If that question has already been asked, he answers the question, offering a different idea.

3.10.13 ACTIVITY DIRECTIONS

3.10.13 ACTIVITY 13 SOCIAL SKILLS GAME

DESCRIPTION	Patients take turns answering questions printed on cards.
OBJECTIVE	To improve self esteem, socialization, and self-expression.
MATERIALS	One large, 6" rubber die. A large hoop. Six brightly colored 3"x 5" cards with one question printed on each card. On the back of the card, draw black dots representing the dots on the die, e.g. question 1 would have one dot on the back, question 2 would have two dots and so on.
SOCIALIZATION QUESTIONS	1. Describe one of your close friends. 2. Where could you meet new people with healthy interests? 3. Tell about a time when you had fun doing something healthy with other people. 4. What healthy social activity could you start doing at discharge? 5. Name two characteristics that you want a good friend to possess. 6. A friend calls and wants to do something, what could you suggest?
DIRECTIONS	Pass the question cards out to six different volunteer patients who take turns rolling the die into the hoop. The patient holding the card with the number of dots showing on the die reads the question and then answers it. The game continues as a second patient rolls the die. If the same number comes up again, the patient holding that card has to give a different answer to that question. Continue with turns until everyone has had a chance to answer a question. A second or third round can be played if the group is small and time allows.

3.10.14 ACTIVITY 14 "Using Sensory Input" Game

DESCRIPTION	A brief description is given of the sensory systems and examples of how they can be used to help with attention and relaxation. Patients take turns throwing a beanbag on poster cards of the sensory systems and discuss how they could use that sense for calming or alerting.
OBJECTIVE	To problem solve how sensory input can be used in everyday situations that will help with self-regulation.
MATERIALS	One beanbag or Koosh. Six brightly colored 8" x 11" poster cards representing the sensory systems of vision, hearing, taste and oral motor activities, smell, touch, and movement (vestibular input and proprioception). Cards consist of the word for the sense and, if possible, a picture representing the sense such as an eye, an ear, a mouth, a nose, a hand, and a person engaged in an exercise activity.
DIRECTIONS	Place the six sense cards on the floor in the center of the circle of patients (they can be in one long row or two rows). Instruct patients to take turns throwing a beanbag or Koosh onto one of the sense cards. Ask the person, whose turn it is, one or two of the following questions: ■ In what ways do you use that sense to help you relax and calm down? ■ Can you think of some new way you can use that sense to help? ■ Is there a way you have used that sense to keep you awake and alert? ■ Is there a way you could use that sense for an activity that could help with sleep? ■ Is there a way that you could use that sense in an activity that helps to combat stress? Patients comment on ways they have used the senses to help in the past and also new ways they could use sensory input in the future.

Copyright © 2005 Karen M. Moore

PART 4

CHAPTER 4: LEVEL II COPING THROUGH THE SENSES GROUP AND INDIVIDUAL TREATMENT

CHAPTER 4A: GROUP TREATMENT

COPING THROUGH THE SENSES
  GROUP PROTOCOL *Handout* **4.1** 85

A LESSON ON COPING THROUGH THE SENSES *Outline* **4.2.1** 87

COPING THROUGH THE SENSES *Worksheet* **4.2.2** 88

COPING THROUGH THE SENSES *Game* **4.3** 89

TUNING INTO THE MIND, BODY AND
  EMOTIONS *Handout* **4.4.1** 90

MAKING POSITIVE CHOICES TO HELP THE MIND, BODY,
  AND EMOTIONS *Worksheet* **4.4.2** 91

CALMING AND ALERTING *Game* **4.5** 92

HELPING OTHERS TO COPE *Worksheet* **4.6** 93

DEVELOPING A STRESS MANAGEMENT PLAN *Worksheet* **4.7** 94

LEARNING GROUNDING TECHNIQUES *Handout* **4.8** 95

DEVELOPING A SENSORY INPUT PLAN *Worksheet* **4.9** 96

LEARNING TO BALANCE WORK, REST
  & PLAN *Worksheet* **4.10** 97

HEALTHY WAYS TO FEEL GOOD *Worksheet* **4.11** 98

Copyright © 2005 Karen M. Moore

CHAPTER 4B: INDIVIDUAL TREATMENT

- **DIRECTIONS FOR BEANBAG TAPPING** *Handout 4.12* 100
- **WORDS FOR BODY STATES AND EMOTIONS** *Handout 4.13* 101
- **SENSATIONAL SELF-CARE** *Handout 4.14* 103
- **SENSORY MENU FOR COPING AND CALMING** *Handout 4.15* 104
- **SENSORY KIT FOR CALMING** *Handout 4.16* 105
- **SENSORY MENU FOR ALERTING** *Handout 4.17* 106
- **DEVELOPING AN ALERTING SNACK BOX** *Handout 4.18* 107
- **LEARNING GROUNDING TECHNIQUES** *Handout 4.8* 95
- **IDENTIFICATION OF AVERSIVE SENSORY STIMULI** *Handout 4.19* 108
- **DEVELOPING A STRESS MANAGEMENT PLAN** *Worksheet 4.7* 94
- **SENSORY MENU FOR STRONG SENSORY INPUT** *Handout 4.20* 109
- **LEARNING TO BALANCE WORK, REST & PLAY** *Worksheet 4.10* 97
- **HEALTHY SLEEP HABITS** *Handout 4.21* 110
- **DEEP BREATHING EXERCISES** *Handout 4.22.1* 111
- **SIMPLE MEDITATION PRACTICES** *Handout 4.22.2* 113
- **DIRECTIONS FOR THE SENSORY DEFENSIVENESS SCREENING FOR ADULTS** *Directions 4.23.1* 116
- **SENSORY DEFENSIVENESS SCREENING FOR ADULTS** *Screening 4.23.2* 117
- **ACUTE CARE TREATMENT PLAN FOR SENSORY DEFENSIVENESS** *Handout 4.23.3* 119

Level II: Coping Through the Senses Group Protocol

Description/Purpose of Group:

This group is designed to build coping and health maintenance skills in patients with mental illness. Patients begin by receiving background information about the sensory systems and learning how to use sensory input for calming and alerting. Group discussions are based on topics related to coping, managing stress, time management, and healthy leisure. Patients learn through the use of worksheets and games that relate to the group topics.

Goals of the Group:

Specific goals from this list will be identified in the patient's treatment plan. Patients will:

1. develop emotional regulation skills.
2. learn positive coping skills to deal with stressful situations, relieve anxiety, manage anger, decrease tension, and avoid self-harm.
3. learn to identify and modify physical and emotional feelings.
4. develop a stress management plan.
5. identify supports and plan for health management.
6. learn grounding techniques to help with dissociation and flashbacks.
7. develop good time management skills to balance work, rest, and play.
8. develop healthy leisure habits.
9. avoid substance abuse.

Membership of Group:

Group size is flexible but this group accommodates 12-14 patients.

Patients who will benefit the most from this group score between 5.0 or higher on the Allen Cognitive Level Screening (ACLS); they need to be able to think abstractly and make plans for the future. Patients must have the self-control and attention span necessary to participate in discussion based group activities for a period of one hour. Patients with the following problems can benefit from this group: mood disorders, depression, anxiety, panic attacks, substance abuse, suicidality, dissociative disorders, Post Traumatic Stress Disorder, self-injurious behaviors, and eating disorders.

Location and Frequency:

This group is conducted for 60 minutes. There are ten topics including education on the senses. The group can be offered as a two-week session held during the five weekdays. If there is a changeover in patients, the ten topics can be repeated. Also, group topics can be interspersed with other topics in a skill-building group designed for the same population. Topics can be chosen according to the goals and

Copyright © 2005 Karen M. Moore

4.1 HANDOUT (page 2 of 2)

needs of the attending patients. The location should be a room large enough to easily accommodate the desk for note taking and writing on the worksheets. A large blackboard is necessary. Pencils should be provided.

Group Leadership:

The group should ideally be co-led by two occupational therapists, unless the group is unusually small (5 or less patients). Students can be trained to co-lead the group with the occupational therapist. The training should include a background on the sensory systems and the use of sensory input strategies.

Methods:

Patients gather in the designated area. Offer a brief explanation of the group topic and remind patients that it is the responsibility of the staff and also group members to maintain confidentiality regarding all group discussions. Introduce staff members and group members.

Pass out the worksheets or materials for a game or other supplies needed for the activity. Specific directions are provided for each of the group topics. Have patients take turns offering responses to questions or offering suggestions to others according to the topic format. Patients can take notes on the worksheets as reminders of ideas, suggestions, and plans accrued during the group.

Leaders take turns with the various aspects of the group or turn the leadership over to patients when it is appropriate. Have one leader serve as a scribe to make notes on patient responses for documentation purposes. Have the other leader also serve as timekeeper to make sure all patients have an opportunity to share their ideas and to assure that the group ends on time.

Close the group by thanking everyone and mention the next time the group will be held.

Coping Through the Senses Group Topics

    Topic 1: A Lesson on Coping Through the Senses
    Topic 2: Coping Through the Senses Game
    Topic 3: Tuning in to the Mind, Body and Emotions
    Topic 4: Calming and Alerting Game
    Topic 5: Helping Others to Cope
    Topic 6: Developing a Stress Management Plan
    Topic 7: Learning Grounding Techniques
    Topic 8: Developing a Sensory Input Plan
    Topic 9: Learning to Balance Work, Rest and Play
    Topic 10: Healthy Ways to Feel Good

Precautions:

Topics in this group can bring up sensitive subjects such as trauma experiences, suicide, and self-harm. Redirect patients from discussing subjects or revealing personal details that could be upsetting to other group members. Offer to meet with the patient later to address their specific concerns.

OUTLINE 4.2.1

A Lesson on Coping Through the Senses

This outline can be used to educate staff or for Topic 1 in the *Coping Through the Senses Group*. Background information can be drawn from Chapter 2 of the Manual. It is designed to be used in conjunction with the *Coping Through the Senses* Worksheet (see 4.2.2). Students may also benefit from receiving the *Calming and Alerting Characteristics of Sensory Input,* Handout (see 2.2).

1. Identification and description of external as well as internal senses

   a. smell/taste
   b. oral/motor input
   c. vision
   d. hearing
   e. light touch
   f. deep pressure touch
   g. proprioception
   h. vestibular sense.

2. General characteristics that make sensory input calming or alerting

   a. Explain the general characteristics of sensory input that could be useful for calming and organizing the body. Input needs to be slow, simple, soft, rhythmic, and have positive associations. Demands need to be low.

   b. Explain general characteristics for sensory input that could be used to alert the system, increase arousal, help with attention, and energize the body. This type of input can be used as a grounding technique. Input needs to be pronounced, quick paced, non-rhythmic, complex, or unexpected. High demands and novelty are useful.

3. Examples of calming and alerting for the individual senses

   a. Ask patients for ideas for calming and alerting and write them on a blackboard using the organization on the Worksheet, *Coping Through the Senses* (see 4.2.2).

   b. Ask students to use the Worksheet to make notes of input ideas specific to their needs.

Copyright © 2005 Karen M. Moore

4.2.2 WORKSHEET

Coping Through the Senses

Activities	**Calming Sensory Input** Used for Stress Reduction, Relaxation, Anxiety	**Alerting Sensory Input** Improve Attention, Grounding, Energizing
SMELL/TASTE		
ORAL MOTOR		
VISION		
HEARING		
TOUCH		
PROPRIOCEPTION		
VESTIBULAR INPUT		

Copyright © 2005 Karen M. Moore

GAME 4.3

COPING THROUGH THE SENSES GAME

DESCRIPTION	Prior to playing this game, patients must receive education regarding the senses (smell/taste, oral motor, vision, hearing, light touch, deep pressure touch, vestibular sense, and proprioception) and the ways sensory input can be used for coping and calming. For this activity, patients answer question cards regarding the use of sensory coping strategies.
OBJECTIVE	Patients will identify personal sensory strategies that could help them to calm down, gain self-control and become grounded or energized in response to stressful situations.
TIME	one hour
MATERIALS	20 brightly colored file cards with the following questions printed on each card regarding the use of sensory techniques. What auditory sensory strategy could you use to calm down? What sensory strategy could you use to keep yourself alert during a boring meeting? Name a deep pressure touch sensory strategy that would be helpful if you are very upset. What sensory strategy could you use to keep yourself alert when driving? Name a sensory strategy that you could use if you are struggling with urges to hurt yourself. Describe something you could use for calming and comfort that involves the sense of smell. Name a grounding technique that involves one of the senses. What activity would <u>you</u> enjoy that involves movement and helps to release the "feel good chemicals" in your body? What movement activity or exercise could you do daily that would help reduce stress? Describe something that is visually upsetting to your system. What sensory strategy could you employ to help you concentrate during an activity? Describe something auditory that is upsetting to your system. Name a sensory strategy that would help to energize you while you are cleaning the house. Name a sensory strategy that could help you get to sleep. Name an activity that uses the vestibular system to help you calm down and relax. What sensory strategy could you use to become more alert during a quick break at your desk? What movement activity could you use to energize yourself? What sensory input could you include in a routine that you use before bedtime to help you relax? Describe a sensory strategy that involves the sense of taste that could alert you or ground you? What sensory strategy could you use in the morning to help you wake up?
DIRECTIONS	Distribute question cards to patients and ask them to answer the questions. Encourage other patients to give comments and suggestions regarding their own experiences in using different sensory strategies.

Copyright © 2005 Karen M. Moore

Tuning Into the Mind, Body and Emotions

Which Word Describes Your Reactions?

HOW ALERT ARE YOU?

Groggy Hypervigilent Distractible	Over stimulated Drowsy Tired	Invigorated Perky Attentive	Lively Energetic Focused

HOW DOES YOUR BODY FEEL PHYSICALLY?

Tense Achy Cool Sweaty Numb Irritated Relaxed	Tight Flaccid Strong Tired Painful Prickly Warm	Lifeless Healthy Weak Swollen Stiff Limp Shaky	Flexible Loose Rigid Comfortable Refreshed Invigorated Exhausted

HOW DOES YOUR STOMACH FEEL PHYSICALLY?

Empty Irritated Nauseous	Full Gassy	Constricted Extended Comfortable	Uncomfortable Knotted

HOW IS YOUR BREATHING?

Normal Deep	Shallow Labored	Wheezy Irregular	

WHAT IS YOUR EMOTIONAL FEELING OR MOOD?

Happy Sad Numb Angry Lonely Upset	Worried Panicky Apathetic Hateful Confident	Excited Confused Peaceful Content Comfortable	Fearful Frustrated Nervous Hopeful Silly

ARE YOU EXPERIENCING ANY OF THESE SIGNS OF STRESS?

Sweatiness Shakiness Nausea Headache	Back pain Tenseness Increased heartbeat Hypertension	Restlessness Disturbed sleep Overtired	Jittery Disturbed appetite Confused

Copyright © 2005 Karen M. Moore

WORKSHEET 4.4.2

Making Positive Choices To Help The Mind, Body And Emotions

Read the 10 events below, one at a time, and then answer each of the following six questions. You can choose from words suggested on the handout "Tuning Into the Mind, Body and Emotions," 4.4.1. Give one example of something you could do to help yourself to feel better in these situations if they are troublesome for you.

How alert are you?
How does your body feel physically?
What sensations do you have in your stomach?
How is your breathing?
What is your emotional feeling or mood?
Do you experience any signs of stress?

EVENTS

1. When you wake up in the Morning

2. When you go to an appointment with your doctor

3. When someone is angry with you

4. When you are angry with someone else

5. When you are working or in your program

6. When you are doing something you enjoy

7. When you are home alone with nothing to do

8. When you have too much to do

9. When you are with a friend

10. When you are in a crowd

Copyright © 2005 Karen M. Moore

4.5 GAME

CALMING AND ALERTING GAME

DESCRIPTION	Prior to playing this game, patients must be taught about the sensory systems (vision, hearing, tasting/oral motor, smell, light touch, deep pressure touch, vestibular sense, and proprioception) and the ways sensory input can be used for coping and calming. Using this information, patients identify ways the senses can be used for the purpose of calming and alerting.
OBJECTIVE	Patients will identify personal sensory strategies that could help them to calm down, gain self-control, and become grounded or energized in response to stressful situations.
TIME	one hour
MATERIALS	19 brightly colored file cards marked accordingly: each card has a word printed on it, representing one of the eight sensory systems. They are: vision, hearing, tasting/oral motor, smell, light touch, deep pressure touch, proprioception, and vestibular. Duplicates are made for each "sense" card; one will have the word "alert" printed on it and the other the word, "calm." Three additional cards are added representing calming for deep pressure touch, proprioception, and vestibular sense.
DIRECTIONS	Distribute the "sense" cards to patients. Lead a discussion by asking each patient to describe how he could use the sensory system represented on the card for calming and alerting as indicated. Encourage patients to share their own experiences and ideas.

Helping Others To Cope

I am having difficulty coping with the following situation or problem:

_____
_____
_____
_____
_____
_____

Suggestions from the Coping Through the Senses Group:

_____
_____
_____
_____
_____
_____
_____
_____
_____
_____
_____
_____
_____

4.7 WORKSHEET

Developing A Stress Management Plan

Incorporate the following suggestions into a plan for stress management.

Be sure to include:

- **At least one movement activity daily emphasizing vestibular or proprioceptive input.** Examples: walking, bicycling, weightlifting, yoga, dancing, and floor exercises. (Use the Sensory Menu for Strong Sensory Input *Handout* 4.20)

- **Pleasurable stimulation in the environment.** Examples: music, chimes, scented candles, room sprays, potpourri, art, bubble lamps, and indoor waterfalls. (Use the Sensory Menu for Coping and Calming *Handout* 4.15 or Suggestions to Enrich Home Environments *Handout* 5.8 in the next chapter.)

- **Weekly routines of sensory enriching leisure activities** such as painting, decorating, playing an instrument, cooking, woodworking, massage, or a bubble bath.

- **Daily deep pressure touch.** Examples: hugs, intimacy, massage, having a pet on the lap, and use of a heavy comforter. (Use Sensory Menu for Strong Sensory Input *Handout* 4.20)

- **Daily deep breathing exercises.** Begin with five minutes, move to ten minutes, and then longer if beneficial. Meditation is encouraged. (Use Deep Breathing Exercises *Handout* 4.22.1 and Simple Meditation Practices *Handout* 4.22.2)

Patient Plan for Stress Management

1. Daily Movement Activities

2. Environmental Enrichment Ideas

3. Plans for Leisure Activities

4. Deep Pressure Touch Alternatives

5. Plans for Deep Breathing or Meditation

List specific ideas that you plan to use for each category.

HANDOUT 4.8

Learning Grounding Techniques

The following sensory input suggestions can breakup or avert a dissociative episode, and help in dealing with flashbacks and panic attacks.

MAKING A PERFUME CANISTER FOR GROUNDING	
EQUIPMENT	Small plastic film canister, cotton balls, strong perfume
DIRECTIONS	Several cotton balls are placed in the film canister. Several drops of a strong perfume are dropped onto the cotton and the cap is replaced making sure it is on tightly.
TO USE	The canister can be kept in a pocket or pocketbook. When a person feels like a dissociative episode is coming on, he or she opens the canister and smells the perfume. If the person is unaware of the episode, a staff member or caregiver can be instructed to remind the person to use the canister when the beginning of a dissociative episode is suspected.

STRONG ALERTING SENSORY INPUT	ACTIVITY IDEAS FOR GROUNDING
Perfume canister	Take a brisk walk
Fireballs/strong mints	Dance to peppy music
Sour balls	Doodle or fidget with something
Chewing large wad of gum	Handle something in pocket like smooth stones
Popsicles	Maintain eye contact with someone
Eating crushed ice	Hold someone's hand
Holding ice	Hold a scented handkerchief to your nose
Snapping elastic on wrist	Focus on one person's voice in a group
Cool fresh air	Write a caring message to yourself
Cool shower	Write or draw in a journal about what is going on
Stamp feet hard	Take a warm bath (Be careful, this could invite dissociation in some people)
Snapping fingers	
Loud clapping	Sing along with a song on the radio
Vigorous exercise	Massage hands or feet with a scented cream (peppermint or lavender is stimulating)
Hopping/skipping/jumping	
	Play solitaire or a video game
	Get involved in a craft project
	Do some heavy work like cleaning or raking
	Do a detailed puzzle
	Color or paint a detailed picture
	Do crossword puzzles or word search puzzles

Copyright © 2005 Karen M. Moore

4.9 WORKSHEET

Developing A Sensory Input Plan

Grounding And Alerting

Sensory input that is highly alerting can be used for grounding and to help prevent dissociation and flashbacks. Alerting sensory input can help with attention and ability to focus on tasks.

List three alerting sensory strategies that would be useful to you:

1. _____

2. _____

3. _____

Coping And Calming

Sensory input can also be useful in a stressful situation or when you might otherwise "fall apart" or lose control or do self-harm.

List three self-composing sensory strategies that you could use to calm yourself:

1. _____

2. _____

3. _____

Stress Management

Activities that give strong organizing sensory input should be done on a regular basis in order to make the body more resilient to stress and to help decrease sensory defensiveness.

List three sensory loaded activities you could do on a regular basis to facilitate health and self-control:

1. _____

2. _____

3. _____

Copyright © 2005 Karen M. Moore

WORKSHEET 4.10

Learning To Balance Work, Rest & Play

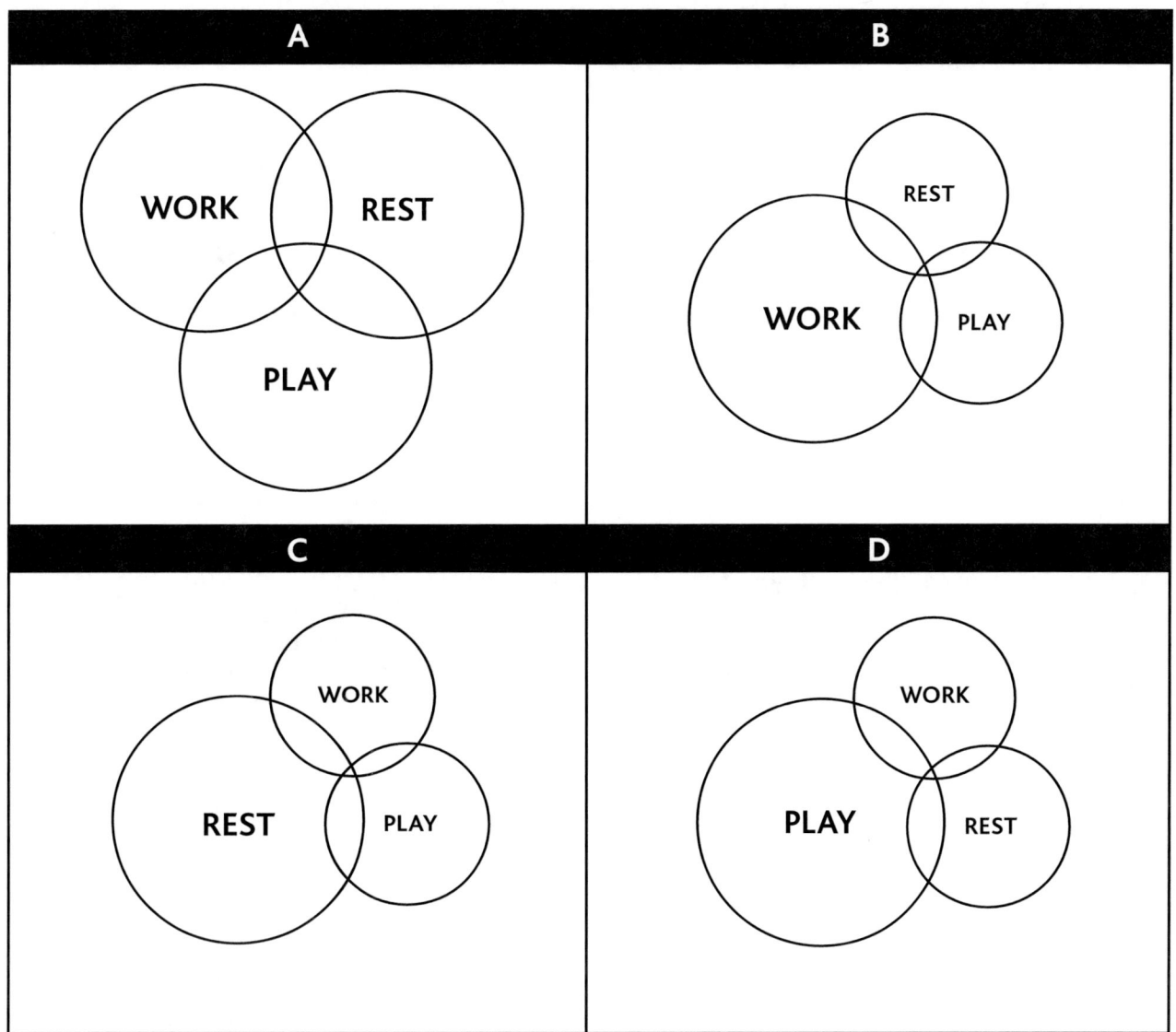

How balanced are you?

On the back of this sheet make lists of things that you do for work, rest, and play.

Are you balanced between work rest and play as in figure A?
Do you have too much work in your life as in figure B?
Do you have too much rest and napping in your life as in figure C?
Do you have too much time to play in your life as in figure D? Is it healthy leisure?

What do you need to change?

Healthy Ways To Feel Good

The following suggestions are offered as ways to feel good by improving health, facilitating relaxation, decreasing anxiety, managing stress, and improving self worth. These ideas can be pursued to stop unhealthy habits such as substance use, addictions, over-eating, over-spending, or over working.

Circle ideas or make notes on the following suggestions that you think would make you feel good in a healthy way and use these ideas to start healthy habits.

1. TAKE SPECIAL CARE OF YOURSELF.

Have a facial	Enjoy a hot tub or Jacuzzi
Get a manicure	Get a haircut or perm
Enjoy a massage	Meditate
Take a whirlpool bath	Have a back rub

2. DEVELOP AN EXERCISE PLAN THAT IS REALISTIC. START SLOWLY. AVOID OVER-EXERTION. FIND EXERCISES THAT YOU ENJOY. EXERCISE TAPS THE BODY'S OWN ARSENAL OF "FEEL GOOD" CHEMICALS.

Jog	Bike	Canoe
Walk	Hike	Kayak
Swim	Skate	Do floor exercise
Lift weights	Surf	Use an exercise video
Use a treadmill		

3. TAKE TIME FOR QUIET RELAXATION.

Listen to music	Write poetry or stories	Play with a pet
Read	Take a nature walk	Listen to Books on tape
Do jigsaw puzzles	Have a cup of tea	Knit or crochet
Draw/paint	Swing in a hammock	Do crossword puzzles
Write in a journal	Rock in a chair or glider	Play solitaire

4. DIRECT MONETARY RESOURCES TO POSITIVE AVENUES SUCH AS MEMBERSHIP IN A GYM, HEALTH CLUB, OR SPORTS CLUB. CONSIDER TAKING A YOGA CLASS OR TRY SOMETHING NEW SUCH AS TAI CHI, KICKBOXING, PILATES, OR KARATE. INVESTING IN A CLASS HELPS WITH CONSISTENCY AND FOLLOW-THROUGH.

5. FIND A HEALTHY LEISURE PURSUIT OR RE-ENGAGE IN FORMER HOBBIES.

Woodworking	Golf	Play cards
Furniture restoration	Sailing	Care for indoor plants
Gardening	Fishing	Mountain biking
Fishing	Hiking	Horseback riding
Quilting	Collection	Snowmobiling
Sewing	Model making	Skiing
Bowling	Flower arranging	Snowshoeing
Crafts	Decorating	Baking
Artwork	Playing an instrument	Gourmet cooking

6. SOCIALIZE - START A SUBSTANCE FREE GAMES GROUP WITH FRIENDS AND MEET WEEKLY TO PLAY CARD GAMES, BOARD GAMES, OR MORE ACTIVE GAMES SUCH AS BOWLING, SOCCER, VOLLEYBALL, OR BOCCE. CONSIDER NEW WAYS TO CONNECT WITH FRIENDS.

Visit a friend	Go to a religious service	Play cards
Go to the library	Do crafts with friends	Play board games
Join a club	Start a cooking group	Have a potluck supper
Go to a sports event	Start a recipe club	Take a class
Go to a movie	Go to a restaurant	Go ballroom dancing
Spend time with your partner	Meet friends for coffee	Go square dancing
Visit a museum	Write to friends	Join a civic club
Visit a nature center	Go to a park concert	Play Bridge

7. CONSIDER A PET. THEY CAN MAKE US LAUGH WHEN NOTHING ELSE SEEMS TO WORK. IF A DOG OR CAT IS TOO MUCH TROUBLE TO TAKE CARE OF, CONSIDER A BIRD, HAMSTER, OR AQUARIUM.

8. MAKE A CONTRIBUTION! HELP SOMEONE. DRAW ON YOUR OWN TALENTS TO LEND A HELPING HAND.

Volunteer in a hospital	Visit someone who is ill	Drive someone to an appointment
Visit a home for the elderly	Help a neighbor	Answer calls for a Hot Line
Teach someone a skill	Coach a team	Be a sponsor
Tutor a child	Help with chores	Help a charity
Volunteer at a museum	Take someone shopping	
Work at a nature center		

Copyright © 2005 Karen M. Moore

4.12 HANDOUT

Directions For Beanbag Tapping

Did you know?

Beanbag tapping is an activity that provides strong deep pressure touch input to the body.

- It helps people become more in touch with the sensations of their own body, especially if the sensory system is disrupted by illness.
- It helps to provide a feeling of "alert calmness" that is a comfortable feeling of being stable, composed, and receptive to conversation and activity.
- The brain craves information and tapping provides good feedback from the receptors of the body helping the sensory system to be more organized and functional.
- It gives a healthy touch experience.
- Taps need to be firm enough to reach the deep pressure touch receptors under the skin.
- Light tapping can be irritating and not calming.

What about the beanbags?

- Beanbags can be purchased from catalogs or stores.
- The size depends on the person, but it should fit comfortably in the hand.
- Small beanbag toys can be substituted if their shape is appropriately comfortable.

HOW TO MAKE A BEANBAG

- Heavy fabrics are best, like denim or corduroy.
- Cut two four inch squares of fabric.
- Place right sides together.
- Sew ½" from the edge around the square leaving a small opening for stuffing.
- Turn right-side out.
- Fill with beans (pea beans, kidney beans, popcorn, or seed corn).
- Hand sew opening.

How to do beanbag tapping:

- Taps should be firm. Tapping should never hurt.
- Taps should be done with an attitude of kindness towards the body.
- Begin by holding the beanbag in one hand.
- Start tapping the opposite hand on both the palm and the back of the hand.
- Work up the arm, experimenting with tapping on various surfaces of the arm.
- Tap shoulders next.
- Then tap across the upper chest on the pectoral muscles.
- Never tap on the neck itself, the face, forehead or stomach!
- Follow up with the opposite hand, arm, and shoulders.
- Tap as much of the back as can be reached comfortably.
- Move on to the legs.
- The thighs, knees, shins, and feet are tapped.
- Tapping feels especially good on the sole of the foot. Make sure you have clean socks.
- When beanbag tapping is finished, stop for a moment to feel how alive and tingly the body feels.

Copyright © 2005 Karen M. Moore

Words For Body States And Emotions

In order to feel less stressed and achieve a state of calm yet alertness, you need to become more aware of body signs and symptoms and more aware of reactions to various events and situations. Words are needed in order to help others know how you are feeling.

This worksheet can serves as a mini diary to keep track of levels of alertness, signs of stress, physical body states, as well as emotional feelings in various situations. Ideally it should be filled out as the day progresses. It only takes a few minutes during the day's activities to tune into the body and select appropriate descriptions. In order to find the right words to describe your reactions, review the handout on *Tuning into the Mind, Body and Emotions* (see 4.4.1).

Waking Up:

Wake up time is _____.

Most Descriptive Words

How alert are you? _____

How does your body feel physically? _____

How does your stomach feel physically? _____

How is your breathing? _____

How is your mood? _____

Describe any signs of stress. _____

Interacting with Others:

The person is _____ and the interaction is _____.

Most Descriptive Words

How alert are you? _____

How does your body feel physically? _____

How does your stomach feel physically? _____

How is your breathing? _____

How is your mood? _____

Describe any signs of stress. _____

Working:

Your work is _____.

Most Descriptive Words

How alert are you? _____

How does your body feel physically? _____

How does your stomach feel physically? _____

How is your breathing? _____

How is your mood? _____

Describe any signs of stress. _____

Copyright © 2005 Karen M. Moore

4.13 WORKSHEET (page 2 of 2)

Doing an Enjoyable Activity:

The activity is _____.

                                                             Most Descriptive Words

How alert are you?   _____

How does your body feel physically?   _____

How does your stomach feel physically?   _____

How is your breathing?   _____

How is your mood?   _____

Describe any signs of stress.   _____

Doing an Activity that you Dislike:

The activity is _____.

                                                             Most Descriptive Words

How alert are you?   _____

How does your body feel physically?   _____

How does your stomach feel physically?   _____

How is your breathing?   _____

How is your mood?   _____

Describe any signs of stress.   _____

Doing Something that takes Concentration:

The activity is _____.

                                                             Most Descriptive Words

How alert are you?   _____

How does your body feel physically?   _____

How does your stomach feel physically?   _____

How is your breathing?   _____

How is your mood?   _____

Describe any signs of stress.   _____

Getting Ready for Bed:

The time is _____.

                                                             Most Descriptive Words

How alert are you?   _____

How does your body feel physically?   _____

How does your stomach feel physically?   _____

How is your breathing?   _____

How is your mood?   _____

Describe any signs of stress.   _____

Copyright © 2005 Karen M. Moore

Sensational Self-Care

Self-care is a personal and rewarding activity that everyone deserves to make a priority. It can be made to be more fun and invigorating by selecting sensory stimulating products and by indulging the body in healthy sensory experiences.

Safety Tip: Allergies can often be problematic, so care must be taken to choose well-tolerated products. Spicy cinnamon, vanilla, and citrus fragrances are sometimes more acceptable that flowery fragrances in patients with allergies. If an initial response is negative, immediately offer an alternative. Patients can have bad associations with particular fragrances. Self-care is very personal, and added care must be taken not to overstep comfort boundaries especially with patients who have been abused.

The following examples are meant to generate even more ideas that are more personal on ways add sensation to everyday self care activities.

- Use fragrant and unusually scented soaps and body washes.
- Teach deep pressure touch input with net bath scrubs or loofa sponges, taking care not to scratch the body. Concentrate on arms and legs and back.
- Try a "foot soak" in Epsom salts.
- Help with a manicure or pedicure with colorful or glittery nail polish.
- Teach a slow hand massage with aromatic hand cream.
- Offer spicy scented shampoos and conditioners.
- Apply body lotion to arms and legs.
- Try a citrus body scrub.
- Give a whirlpool bath.
- Furnish an aromatic drink such as coffee or herbal tea while performing hygiene routine.
- Play music during self-care.
- Help a person color their hair.
- Brush hair well and arrange hair.
- Massage scalp or indulge in a hot oil treatment for dry brittle hair.
- Try an herbal facial treatment.
- Use tasty lip-gloss.
- Have a mini makeup party.
- Help with shaving.
- Offer spicy scented shaving creams.
- Provide fragrant after-shave cologne.
- Rub the body briskly with a towel before and after a shower.
- Hold a warm facecloth to the face to let moisture sink in.
- Try a refreshing mouthwash or new flavored toothpaste.
- Spray the air with a refreshing room fragrance before hygiene routine.

Copyright © 2005 Karen M. Moore

4.15 HANDOUT

Sensory Menu For Coping And Calming

Review the following suggestions, and note those that you think would be helpful to you in stressful situations. Plan specific ways to use them. Find ways to integrate calming sensory input into everyday routines.

- Routines
- Familiarity
- Low demands
- Scented candle
- Hand massage
- Body massage
- Warmth
- Soft slow rhythmic music
- Slow rhythmic movement
- Rocking self back and forth
- Rocking chair/glider
- Swinging
- Tuck sheets in tightly at bedtime
- Blanket wraps
- Soft voices
- Apply gentle pressure to shoulders
- Weighted lap pad
- Heavy stuffed or real animal on lap
- Stroking an animal
- Watching an aquarium
- Background noise of bubbling water
- Fountain or aquarium filter
- Rhythmic sound of a fan
- Sound of ocean waves
- Hugs and self hugs
- Sleep in sleeping bag
- Firm pressure on shoulders
- Warm bath
- Back rub
- Watch flickering fire
- Rhythmic bouncing of ball
- Color or paint something easy
- Work with clay or play dough
- Foot roller
- Taking time out for quiet
- Deep breathing
- Meditation
- Yoga
- Humming, singing quietly
- Rhythmic counting
- Head rolls (back and forth)
- Walking slowly
- Imagine favorite scene
- Ride in a car
- Sit in the sun
- Sit on hands or legs
- Relaxation tapes
- Chewing gum
- Squeezing stress ball
- Sucking on lollipop or something sweet
- Slow stroking on back
- Warm drink
- Dim light
- Slow graceful dancing
- Pastel colors

Copyright © 2005 Karen M. Moore

Sensory Kit For Calming

Assemble a selection of items in a box, basket, or suitcase that can be kept handy for patient or staff.

- Scented hand cream
- Cedar filled mini pillow
- Beanbag
- Stress Ball
- Gum
- Lollipops or hard candies to suck
- Hand/foot roller
- Crossword puzzle or word games
- Theraband for rowing
- Koosh balls
- Relaxation music
- Blanket to wrap up in
- Book with beautiful pictures

Copyright © 2005 Karen M. Moore

Sensory Menu For Alerting

Review the list of suggestions below, and note those that could be helpful to you for concentrating and attending. Consider different situations when these ideas could be used.

- Novelty
- High demands
- Perfume canister
- Fireballs/strong mints
- Sour balls
- Chewing large wad of gum
- Spicy food
- Crunchy snacks
- Holding ice
- Cold drink
- Snapping elastic on wrist
- Cool room
- Bright colors
- Fresh air
- Brisk walk
- Bright light
- Loud or lively music/irregular beat
- Dancing to peppy music
- Brush feather or Koosh on face
- Loud voices
- Doodling
- Snapping fingers
- Loud clapping
- Shifting weight in chair
- Yawning
- Whistle or hum
- Drum or tap fingers
- Fidget toys
- Hopping/skipping
- Wake up stretch
- Vigorous exercise
- Cool shower
- Fiddling with hair or jewelry
- Handling something in pocket
- Stand to work at counter
- Kneel-stand to work
- Stamp feet hard
- Sucking on a Popsicle
- Eating crushed ice

HANDOUT 4.18

Developing An Alerting Snack Box

Any suitable box, bag, or pocketbook can be used, depending on the need of portability or need to conceal items. Additional ideas can be added by using the Sensory Menu for Alerting *Handout* (see 4.17).

Suggested Items:

- Perfume to dab on the wrist
- Lemon drops
- Fireballs
- Strong mints
- Crunchy cereal Crunchy snack
- CD or tape player and lively music
- Koosh ball to manipulate
- Stress ball
- Fidget widgets
- Smooth stones to manipulate
- Perfume canister

Additional Ideas:

Copyright © 2005 Karen M. Moore

Identification Of Aversive Sensory Stimuli

Use this list to identify sensory experiences that are stressful or uncomfortable to you. Make a plan to avoid, minimize or prepare for this aversive sensory stimulation.

- Certain smells
- Certain foods
- Foods with mixed textures
- Foods with strong flavors
- Mushy foods
- Chewing
- Noisy places
- Quiet places
- Background noise
- Distracting sounds
- White noise
- Certain kinds of music
- Relaxation tapes
- Unexpected noises
- Radio talk
- Several people talking at the same time
- Dim light
- Bright light
- Florescent light
- Flickering light
- Fast moving images
- Scanning text
- Watching T.V.
- Getting dressed
- Getting undressed
- Showering or bathing
- Washing face
- Brushing teeth
- Hair being combed, washed, cut
- Touching messy substances
- Tight clothing
- Loose clothing
- Wearing a hat
- Bare skin
- Sweating
- Being in unfamiliar places
- Walking barefoot
- Sensitivities to clothing textures
- New clothing
- Pulling shirt or jacket over head
- Being touched by others
- Holding hands
- Intimate touch
- Hugs
- People standing too close
- Being in a group
- Being in a crowd
- Closed rooms
- Being outside
- Being alone
- Riding in a car
- Shopping
- Waiting in lines
- Being around people
- Difficulty with chaotic environments
- Changes in routine
- Having to sit still
- Certain time of day
- Sudden changes in motion or direction
- Transfers
- Getting up from a chair
- Fear of falling
- Spinning or turning
- Walking on stairs
- Walking on bumpy surfaces
- Upset by movement activities
- Exercising
- Being cold or hot
- Being around people
- Having to sit still
- Being in unfamiliar places

HANDOUT 4.20

Sensory Menu For Strong Sensory Input

These activities can become the core of a stress management plan. One item from each category should be done on a daily basis. Choose a different activity each day. These are all example activities; many other exercises are available. Use judgment and reason when performing these activities. Consult with your physician regarding strenuous physical exercise.

DEEP PRESSURE TOUCH

- Full body massage – provided by a trained professional
- Hand and foot massage (with or without rollers) for three minutes each
- Bean bag tapping – a beanbag is used to give slow firm taps on hands, arms, shoulders, upper back and legs– three minute total
- Sit with something heavy in the lap – heavy lap quilt or animal
- Back rub or slow stroking – a trusted person uses slow firm pressure to rub back or stroke down alternating sides of the spinal cord

VESTIBULAR INPUT ACTIVITIES

- Swinging
- Rocking in chair or glider – for 15 – 30 minutes
- Head rolls/side rocking – Roll head slowly from shoulder to shoulder 10X; follow by rocking side to side in chair – repeat
- Movement exercises - such as those in routine for Sense-abilities Group - 10 min.
- Rowing machine – strong proprioceptive input also
- Dancing/jazzercise
- Swimming – good for all 3 types of input
- Exercise band rowing – hook well knotted ring of heavy exercise band over foot; rock back while pulling on band, rock forward – repeat in rowing type motion – 10X then stop to breath deeply– repeat 3X

PROPRIOCEPTIVE INPUT ACTIVITIES

- Chewing large wad of gum
- Walking
- Jogging
- Heavy work (raking, moving furniture)
- Treadmill
- Nordic Track
- Bicycling
- Life cycle
- Yoga
- Martial Arts
- Trampoline jumping
- Volleyball
- Aerobic exercise
- Stair master or climber
- Jumping rope
- Water exercises or aerobics
- Floor exercises
- Golf
- Chair push-ups
- Weight lifting
- Ping-pong and badminton
- Baseball and softball
- Tennis and squash

Copyright © 2005 Karen M. Moore

Healthy Sleep Habits

- Establish a consistent sleep-wake schedule
- Avoid daytime naps
- Exercise daily (5-6 hrs. before bedtime)
- Avoid caffeine and foods that distress the stomach
- Reserve bedroom for sleep only
- Pick a certain time at night when you will stop working, planning, and worrying and relax!
- Set up bedtime routine
- Have milk and crackers or a light snack
- Try foot flexes before bedtime
- Take a warm bath before retiring
- Use scented oils or candles as a part of the routine
- Give your hands or feet a massage
- Try yoga or meditation in the evening
- Play restful music
- Try reading something pleasurable before bed
- Use a heavy coverlet
- Use a heating pad, hot water bottle, or electric blanket to provide soothing warmth
- Wear socks to bed to avoid cold feet
- Run a fan for "white noise"
- If you lie in bed for more than 15 minutes without falling asleep, get up and engage in a quiet activity until sleepy

Lack of sleep can cause:

- ✔ Decreased cognitive capacities
- ✔ Decreased perceptual abilities
- ✔ Slow motor responses
- ✔ Diminished interests
- ✔ Lost work and poor performance
- ✔ Danger in the workplace
- ✔ Dangerous driving
- ✔ Increased agitation
- ✔ Symptoms that mimic depression

Deep Breathing Exercises

Deep breathing, also called diaphragmatic breathing, is the most basic relaxation exercise. By breathing slowly and deeply from the abdomen a person can enter a deep state of relaxation anywhere, anytime, with no special equipment or training. It works best if it is practiced on a daily basis. Even a few breaths can help the body to calm down. Ideally you should work up to ten and then twenty minutes of deep breathing each day.

Make yourself comfortable. You can lie down on your back with the head supported by a pillow and possibly another pillow under the knees. One drawback to this position is that people fall asleep. This can be used to your advantage at night, but it is not a full deep breathing experience unless you remain focused on the breathing. You can also sit in the lotus position with the legs crossed in front or in a semi lotus position with one leg extended. Sitting on a pillow makes this position more comfortable for some people. You can also sit in a chair. It is important to be comfortable.

- *Close your eyes and put your hands gently on the stomach in order to feel the breaths. Inhale deeply through the nose feeling the abdomen expand as you breathe in. Pause, and then slowly exhale with your mouth and lips puckered as if blowing bubbles. That helps to slow down the breathing. Exhale until the lungs feel empty.*

- *Continue to breathe in and out slowly and deeply—in through the nose and out through pursed lips. Make sure the stomach expands and contracts with the breaths; if the shoulders rise and fall instead, your breathing is still shallow and only expanding the chest area.*

- *One way to make the breaths more rhythmic is to count to four slowly as you inhale, pause, and them exhale slowly to the count of four.*

- *Focus on your breathing. When your thoughts wander, just bring them back to focus on the breathing. If worries come into your mind, just set them aside and refocus. This becomes easier with practice.*

Copyright © 2005 Karen M. Moore

■ *Each time you breathe out, try to relax the body a little bit more. If a particular area is tense, focus on relaxing it as you exhale.*

■ *Continue to breathe for just a few minutes or as long as twenty minutes. When ready to stop, open your eyes slowly and continue a few more breaths and remain still for a few minutes before returning to other activities.*

■ *The more you practice, the more helpful the breathing exercises will become. It is easier to utilize them in times of stress if you have practiced regularly.*

Guided Deep Breathing

To add another dimension of sensation and focus to the breathing routine some "feeling words" can be added to the practice. Guiding words are suggested in the text box. Each pair of phrases can be repeated three times, for a total of nine deep breaths.

GUIDED BREATHING EXERCISES

Breathing in, I know I am breathing in.

Breathing out, I know I am breathing out

Breathing in, I feel my body.

Breathing out, I calm my body.

Smiling to my body, I breathe in.

Releasing tension in my body, I breathe out.

by Thich Hanh Nhat

Simple Meditation Practices

Sensory Awareness Meditation

Set aside a ten or twenty minute time for practice, daily if possible. Explain to others in the household that this is part of your plan for good health and ask if they could refrain from disturbing you during this time.

Sit in a very comfortable position. Put a pillow behind you for support if needed. Keep legs uncrossed. Use a stool for the feet if it is more comfortable. You may want to bring something very tiny for the taste meditation such as a raisin, or chocolate chip, or piece of carrot. You may also want to rub some scented hand cream into your hands to enhance the smell and touch meditations.

Relax!!! Take a very deep breath and give a big sigh as you exhale. Push away thoughts of your daily concerns. There will be plenty of time for them later. This is time to take a vacation from your troubles. Take another breath and sigh it out envisioning your tension going out with the breath.

Begin by focusing on your breath for at least ten breaths. If necessary, keep your hand on your abdomen to feel it expand and contract in order to make sure you are doing deep abdominal breathing.

As you breathe repeat these words to yourself: I breathe in deeply.
I breathe out s-l-o-w-l-y.

Once your deep breathing is comfortable and natural, turn your attention to your sensory experiences.

Become aware of what you see around you. Focus on the details. Notice things you have been too busy to notice before. Consider variations in colors, textures, forms, and shapes. Scan slowly and deliberately.

Become aware of things you hear. Listen first to the sound of your breath. What else do you hear? Notice subtle things like the buzz of the refrigerator, the hum of traffic, the sounds of insects. Are the sounds you hear pleasant, interesting, rhythmic, or sporadic?

If you have music in the background, pay careful attention to the melodies and variations in tempo and volume.

Become aware of any smells. Can you smell your own hand cream or after shave lotion? Can you smell something cooking? Does your home have a special smell? Can you smell cleaning products or polish? Do any smells remain from pets, or children, or activities such as woodworking?

Become aware of any sensations of taste. These can be residual toothpaste or flavors leftover from tea or dessert or a salty snack. Lick your lips. Is there any taste? If you have come prepared with something to taste, lick and consume it very, very slowly noticing as much about it as you can. Play with it in your mouth. Notice variations in textures.

Focus on touch. First, focus on the feelings of your body as it contacts the chair and the stool. Feel your clothing. Slowly massage your hands feeling each area. Begin a body scan and feel your scalp

Copyright © 2005 Karen M. Moore

and hair. Move your focus slowly to your head, then neck, then shoulders, and slowly down one arm at a time. Note any areas of tension. Consciously relax that area; sometimes it helps to contract the muscles and then feel them relax. If there is pain, just acknowledge it and move on. Move your focus down your torso and the back and then to the hips and pelvic area and then slowly down each leg to the feet and even the toes. Feel the environment. Is there a breeze? Feel the temperature.

Lastly, become very aware and alert to everything. Try to take in a general sense of the feelings of your whole body and the sensations of the environment around you.

End the meditation by returning your focus to your breathing.

SENSORY AWARENESS MEDITATION

Relax!!! Take a very deep breath and give a big sigh as you exhale.

Begin by focusing on your breath for at least ten breaths.

As you breathe repeat these words to yourself. I breathe in deeply.
I breathe out s-l-o-w-l-y.

Become aware of what you see around you.

Become aware of things you hear.

Become aware of any smells.

Become aware of any sensations of taste.

Focus on touch.

Lastly, become very aware and alert to everything.

End the meditation by returning your focus to your breathing.

Sensory Walking Meditation

This meditation can be done daily, especially if you ordinarily walk daily anyway. It can be alternated with the sitting meditation. They are very similar. This simple routine can last ten to twenty minutes. You may want to tuck a smooth stone in your pocket to feel as well as something small to taste and smell if you do not anticipate finding things along the way. Allow a few minutes before you start to let the concerns and worries of the day settle down.

Relax!!! Take a very deep breath and give a big sigh as you exhale.

Begin by focusing on your breath for at least ten breaths. If necessary, keep your hand on your abdomen to feel it expand and contract in order to make sure you are doing deep abdominal breathing.

As you breathe repeat these words to yourself.　I breathe in deeply.
**　　　　　　　　　　　　　　　　　　　　　　I breathe out s-l-o-w-l-y.**

Once your deep breathing is comfortable and natural turn your attention to your sensory experiences.

Become aware of what you see around you. Focus on the details. Notice the sky. Look closely at the vegetation. Notice the ground you are walking on. Notice the houses, playground sets, dogs, or people as you pass. Notice things your have been too busy to notice before. Scan slowly and deliberately.

Become aware of things you hear. Listen first to the sound of your breath. What else do you hear? Notice subtle things like the songs of the birds, insect noises or the chirps of a chipmunk. Can you hear the rain or the wind? Listen to your footsteps. Are the sounds you hear pleasant, interesting, rhythmic, or sporadic?

Become aware of any smells. Does the air have any special smell? Can you smell wood burning or someone using the grille? Can you smell any flowers? Pick up a leaf, flower, piece of grass, or herb from a garden; does it have a smell?　　If you have brought along something to smell, manipulate it in your hand to bring out the aroma.

Become aware of any sensations of taste. These can be residual toothpaste, or flavors leftover from tea or dessert or a salty snack. Is there anything safe to taste as you walk along like sweet grass, mint, or snow? If you have come prepared with something to taste, lick and consume it very, very slowly noticing as much about it as you can. Play with it in your mouth. Notice variations in textures.

Focus on touch. First, focus on the feelings of your body as you move. Begin by focusing on your feet as they strike the pavement. Slowly work your attention up your legs, feeling the ankles, knees, and then hips. Feel your back. Is it tense? If you find tension, contract and relax the muscles to release the tension. Can you feel your abdomen expand as you breathe? Move your focus up to your shoulders and then down one arm at a time. Slowly massage your hands feeling each area. Move your focus to your neck. Do a couple of slow gentle neck roles to help release any tension. Feel your face, tense and release your jaw, blink several times, wiggle your nose, scrunch your face. Next feel your scalp and hair. Feel your clothing as it touches you when you move. Feel the environment. Is there a breeze? Feel the temperature.

Lastly, become very aware and alert to everything. Try to take in a general sense of the feelings of your whole body and the sensations of the environment around you.

End the meditation by returning your focus to your breathing.

Copyright © 2005 Karen M. Moore

4.23.1 DIRECTIONS

SENSORY DEFENSIVENESS SCREENING FOR ADULTS

The Sensory Defensiveness Screening for Adults, composed of two parts, is used to determine if a patient is experiencing symptoms associated with sensory defensiveness and, if so, how it is affecting functional performance and relationships.

DIRECTIONS	In Part 1, the patient checks Yes or No beside a behavior associated with sensory defensiveness (e.g., do you avoid noisy places). Ask the patient if he has any questions regarding the items. For example, many patients have questions about addictive behaviors (which include substance abuse, gambling, and food addictions). Explain that a "Yes" response refers to a behavior that occurs often or has been a recent problem. If the behavior occurred a long time ago, but not recently, the answer is No. If the characteristic applies infrequently, the answer is No.
	Begin Part II by explaining that the purpose of this section is to determine if those sensory defensive behaviors checked YES in Part I are having an impact on the patient's everyday functioning (e.g., socialization, hygiene, leisure). Functional problems can be the result of many factors, but for the purpose of this screening, the problem must be due to sensory related issues. For example, patients may be depressed and withdrawing from all social relationships. If they are avoiding others and it is not due to discomfort from touch or other symptoms related to sensory defensiveness, then they would circle N on the fifth functional situation addressing socialization. A patient may not realize that social withdrawal is due to sensory issues. If that patient has identified many behaviors in Part I, further investigation is suggested.
	To further understand the patient's sensory processing, a short history is taken. At the end of Part II there is a short list of experiences, highly associated with sensory defensiveness, for the patient to check. A person with a history of these experiences does not necessarily have a sensory defensive problem but special attention should be taken on the part of the therapist to make sure these patients are not exhibiting sensory defensive symptoms.
	The results must be interpreted by an Occupational Therapist familiar with Sensory Defensiveness. If the patient identifies a significant number of behaviors and if those behaviors are impacting patient function, further assessment is recommended.

SENSORY DEFENSIVENESS SCREENING FOR ADULTS

Name: _____ Date: _____ Circle: Male or Female

Age: _____ Circle: Patient Staff Student Other Occupation: _____

Diagnosis: _____ Living situation: _____

PART I

Please score first and immediate response by circling
Y (if behavior usually applies) or **N (if behavior rarely applies)**.

Do you:

- Y N   layer your clothing often
- Y N   overdress for the temperature
- Y N   prefer long sleeves, even in summer
- Y N   pick illogical clothing preferences
- Y N   repeatedly wear favorite clothes
- Y N   experience discomfort with dressing or undressing
- Y N   get irritated by showering
- Y N   get irritated by face washing, or shaving
- Y N   get irritated by tooth brushing
- Y N   have poor personal hygiene
- Y N   like wrapping yourself in bedding
- Y N   sit with hands or feet underneath you
- Y N   bite hand/wrist/arm when upset
- Y N   bang head or part of body when upset
- Y N   grind teeth
- Y N   prefer to touch rather than be touched
- Y N   become upset when someone comes behind you
- Y N   find touch to be painful/ harmful
- Y N   get anxious when being hugged
- Y N   like an exaggerated personal space
- Y N   find that closed rooms bother you
- Y N   avoid crowded places
- Y N   startle more easily than others
- Y N   have patterns of social withdrawal
- Y N   have unexplained emotional outbursts
- Y N   feel you are always "on guard"

Do you:

- Y N   avoid food with mixed textures
- Y N   have difficulty swallowing
- Y N   like noxious odors (gasoline, etc.)
- Y N   seem overly sensitive to smells
- Y N   avoid noisy places
- Y N   need absolute quiet to concentrate
- Y N   get agitated by white noise (fan, etc.)
- Y N   get irritated by sounds others would ignore
- Y N   have trouble staying on the line when reading/writing
- Y N   get overly bothered by lights at night
- Y N   get distraught by occluded vision (such as a blindfold)
- Y N   become upset by complex visual stimuli (lots of colors or moving objects)
- Y N   find yourself staring at things
- Y N   over-react to unstable surfaces
- Y N   often bump into things
- Y N   lose balance easily
- Y N   rock back and forth to calm yourself
- Y N   dislike heights
- Y N   fatigue easily
- Y N   feel uncomfortable with body or looks
- Y N   cut or hurt self when anxious or upset
- Y N   not feel pain
- Y N   dislike routine
- Y N   exhibit addictive behaviors

Score Section I: # Y _____   # N _____   out of 50 items   % Yes _____

Copyright © 2005 Karen M. Moore

4.23.2 SCREENING (page 2 of 2)

PART II
Functional Implications

First, consider the sensory behaviors that you checked "Yes" in Part I.

Then, thinking about the sensory behaviors, read each of the questions below. Circle **Y for yes** or **N for no** beside each question. If the question does not apply to you, write NA. Note: Do not respond with yes if these problems are caused by something other than sensory problems. For example poor hygiene could be due to fatigue caused by depression, not because bathing is irritating.

Please explain answer if it is YES.

Y N   Do these sensory behaviors interfere with your **hygiene** and your ability to dress and care for yourself the way you would like?

Y N   Do these sensory behaviors prevent you from being **independent** in the community (driving, going to public places)?

Y N   Do these sensory behaviors interfere with your **relationships** with other people?

Y N   Do these sensory behaviors interfere with your ability to enjoy an **intimate relationship**?

Y N   Do these sensory behaviors interfere with your ability to **socialize** with others?

Y N   Do these sensory behaviors interfere with your ability to **care for your home or your family**?

Y N   Do these sensory behaviors interfere with your ability to go to **school** or to perform your **job** or to seek employment?

Y N   Do these sensory behaviors interfere with your ability to enjoy **leisure** activities and to have fun?

Y N   Do these sensory behaviors interfere with your **safety**?

Check any experiences that apply:

____History of sexual abuse   ____Respiratory problems   ____Serious injury or surgery

____History of physical abuse ____Multiple hospitalizations   ____Traumatic birth

____Self-harming behavior   ____Torture   ____Suicide attempts

____Eating disorder   ____Serious stomach problems   ____Period of sensory deprivation

HANDOUT 4.23.3

Acute Care Treatment Plan For Sensory Defensiveness

1. Have the patient complete The *Sensory Defensiveness Screening for Adults*. If a significant number of behaviors are identified that interfere with life roles, the patient is then interviewed to obtain a comprehensive sensory history and involvement in valued life roles and activities.

2. Teach the patient about Sensory Defensiveness and the importance of a healthy sensory diet. Discuss the sensory systems and they contribute to function in negative or positive ways. Stress the significance of deep pressure touch, proprioception, and vestibular input.

3. Use the sensory menus in this chapter to help the patient identify aversive stimuli and situations. Discuss coping strategies and environmental changes.

4. Have the patient identify useful sensory input for grounding, alerting and calming. Discuss ways to implement their use in daily routines.

5. Have the patient identify preferred deep pressure touch and movement from the menu. He should participate in two movement activities daily, one that emphasizes vestibular input and one that emphasizes proprioceptive input. Recommend that deep pressure touch input is incorporated into daily routines.

6. Suggest to the patient that he does beanbag tapping regularly throughout the day for a total of four or more times, performing slowly and with firm pressure on the hands, arms, shoulders, back, and legs and avoiding the head and abdomen areas. One month of this activity is sufficient. Beanbag tapping can be used on an "as needed basis" to avoid self-harming behaviors.

7. Encourage the patient to keep a small journal to record sensory rich activities each day as well as the number of times beanbag tapping is performed. Ask the patient to identify two troublesome symptoms related to sensory defensiveness such as isolation, self-harm, or avoidance of housework. He should keep track of these symptoms by estimating the number of times or minutes spent doing or not doing problematic behaviors.

8. Encourage the patient to report to the occupational therapist if the symptoms increase or lessen and if the activities are helpful. If so, how?

Copyright © 2005 Karen M. Moore

PART 5

CHAPTER 5: ENVIRONMENTAL SUPPORT

CREATING A SENSORY BOX *Handout* 5.1 123

STRATEGIES TO AVOID THE USE OF RESTRAINTS *Handout* 5.2. 124

ACUTE INTERVENTIONS FOR SELF-INJURIOUS BEHAVIORS *Handout* 5.3 . . . 125

DEVELOPING A SENSORY ROOM *Handout* 5.4 126

SUGGESTIONS FOR DAY ROOM SPACE *Handout* 5.5 127

RECOMMENDATIONS FOR HOSPITAL ENVIRONMENTS *Handout* 5.6 128

SAFE SPACE *Handout* 5.7 129

SUGGESTIONS TO ENRICH HOME ENVIRONMENTS *Handout* 5.8 130

HELPING PATIENTS WITH COGNITIVE DEFICITS *Handout* 5.9 131

Copyright © 2005 Karen M. Moore

HANDOUT 5.1

Creating A Sensory Box

The Sensory Box is a compilation of supplies for sensory activities that is readily available for the use of patients, caregivers, and staff members. A rolling suitcase is a handy container. Activities can be used to help patients with anxiety, panic attacks, dissociative incidents, suicidality, problems with self-control, self-injurious behaviors, and to avoid physical restraints. Resources for the supplies can be found in Appendix A of the Manual.

Smell
Evening Spa (4 scents along with 6 sounds like Spring Rain and Woodlands)
Aromatherapy Scents, Aromatic Room Sprays or Assortment of Room Freshener Tags
Perfume Canister
Scented hand and body lotions

Taste and Oral Motor
Cinnamon Hot Balls, Hard Candies or Gum
Crunchy or Chewy Food Items (bag of pretzels or chips, licorice twists)

Auditory
CD Player and Selection of Relaxation CD's
Environments (8 quieting natural sounds 30 min and 60 Segments; battery operated)
Soothing Time Audio Relaxer (30 nature sounds; battery operated)
Envirascape Soothing Indoor Wind Chime

Visual
Water Colors (Changing glass sphere of light with nature sounds; battery operated)
Glow in the Dark Color Sand Picture or Sandbuilder (Cascading Sand in round frame)
Books of Art, Animals or Scenery

Deep Pressure Touch
Weighted Blanket, Weighted Lap Pad or Vest
Body Sense NeckEase Weighted Pillow (can be warmed in microwave or refrigerated)
Theraband Hand Exercisers (can be heated or frozen)
Beanbags
Hand, foot, or back rollers

Vestibular
Vibrating Bug (Innocently shaped massager) or Vibrating Pillows

Proprioception
Exercise "Loops" (great for exercise band rowing)

Fidget Widgets
Assortment of Koosh Balls
Squish Balls, Knead-A-Ball or other stress balls
Tangle

Activities
Playing cards, Puzzles or Word Games
Intricate coloring projects
Inspirational Books
Deep Breathing Instructions

Copyright © 2005 Karen M. Moore

5.2 HANDOUT

Strategies To Avoid The Use Of Restraints

- Use deep pressure touch to calm and help gain self-control. Obtain deep pressure through the use of a weighted blanket, heavy lap pad, or weighted stuffed animal.

- Provide overall deep pressure by using the strategy of "tight tucking." Have the patient lie on the bed covered with a sheet or sheet and blanket reaching over the shoulders, but not over the neck or head area. The sheet(s) are then tucked in on three sides providing firm pressure to the person's body. Patients accept tight tucking well, and it is very calming. This provides gentle external pressure that is much more normal than a restraint.

- Have the patient rock slowly in a rocking chair. Slow linear rocking is one of the fastest ways to calm a person down.

- Teach patients to wrap themselves up tightly in a blanket by bringing it around their back, crossing it in front of them and holding it snugly with the hands.

- Give the patient mitts for the self-injurious behaviors of picking or scratching. Some mitts are even designed to isolate the fingers.

- Have the patient manipulate or squeeze something in their hands as a way to interrupt self-injurious behaviors.

- Use physical holding restraints, as they are not as intrusive to the patient as the typical restraints. For a two-person restraint, two staff members stand on opposite sides of the sitting patient. The person on the patient's left takes the patient's right arm and crosses it firmly over the body, with the hand being held tight to the patient's left thigh. The person on the right does the opposite, crossing the left arm in front and holding it against the right thigh. Give gentle full body pressure against the sides of the patient; talk calmly to the patient, focusing on safety and control and not on the behavior. Say, "Calm down; we are here to help you stay safe. Take a deep breath." If the situation is not critical perform a one-person physical holding restraint by standing behind the patient. Grasp the patient's hands and cross both arms in front of the body, holding both hands tightly to the thighs. Often the patient calms down quickly, and the physical restraint can be released.

- Distract the patient with a valued activity such as a craft or a puzzle to interrupt the unwanted behavior.

- Engage the patient in a helping task involving heavy work patterns that are calming. Examples include moving furniture, raking, and vacuuming.

- Teach the patient who frequently ends up in restraint a repertoire of helpful calming sensory input strategies to use as soon as they become agitated or upset.

- Invite the patient to a quiet place where a selection of soothing sensory input is available. This can be a "sensory room" or a place set aside with equipment such as a rocking chair and a *Sensory Box* with weighted blankets and lap pads, soothing music, candies to suck on and gum, and fidget widgets.

Acute Interventions For Self-Injurious Behaviors

Early intervention is most effective with self-injurious behaviors. The following questions can help identify signs that a patient is at risk for self-harm.

What situations cause the patient extreme discomfort that can lead to harm?

What symptoms have preceded self-injury in the past?

Suggested Interventions

- Bring the person to a safe and quiet space where behaviors can be monitored.

- Provide strong sensory input in the hospital environment through chair pushups, exercise band rowing, joint compression, performance of gentle head rolls, or chewing a large ward of gum.

- Encourage the use of rocking in a chair or glider.

- Use beanbag tapping (works well on the arms in lieu of self-injury there – monitor to prevent harmful tapping).

- Try a regime of beanbag tapping every few hours.

- Provide deep pressure touch such as "hand hugs" (clasp both hands around patient's hand and give firm pressure. Continue clasping by moving to the wrist, then up the arm to the shoulder. Repeat with the other arm, if tolerated).

- Place something heavy on the lap, preferably something to stroke such as corn filled stuffed animals or a heavy pillow covered with a fuzzy fabric.

- Try holding the person's hand as a gesture of care and concern along with sensory feedback.

- Engage the patient in helper tasks that involve "heavy work" such as carrying boxes or moving chairs.

- Provide something to manipulate in the hand such as a stress ball or "fidget widget."

- Put mitts on hands and then substitute snug gloves.

- Engage the patient in activity such as crafts or card playing.

Copyright © 2005 Karen M. Moore

5.4 HANDOUT

Developing A Sensory Room

Supplies for a Sensory Room (Recommended)
Resources for these products can be found in Appendix A of the Manual.

- Cassette player and relaxing music
- Well stocked *Sensory Box*
- Beanbags for tapping
- Fan to blow cool air
- Dimmer for lights
- Exercise band for rowing
- Therapy Balls
- Light blanket to wrap up in
- Beanbag chairs or Foof Chair
- Rockers or gliders
- Mobiles
- Posters of nature scenes
- Bubble or lava lamps or fiber optic spray
- Artificial aquarium or small indoor water fountain
- Aromatic room sprays
- Stress balls and Koosh balls
- Items to touch and manipulate (fidget widgets)
- Warm coverlets
- Weighted lap pads
- Heavy corn filled stuffed animal (Heavy Duty Dog)
- Items to taste or chew or crunch
- Hand held vibrating massager
- Hand and foot rollers
- Hammock or suspended swing
- Life Cycle or piece of exercise equipment
- Exercise mats
- Books on self-help, inspiration, nature, art

The Sensory Room is used as a ...

- place for leisure where patients go to relax and enjoy pleasant sensory stimulation such as beautiful music and something interesting to view.
- quiet environment for patients to chill out and regain composure.
- private place where sensory input modalities can be used for emotional regulation and to work on self-awareness.
- place to calm patients down to avoid restraint.
- setting for sensory related groups including the *Sense-ability Group* or the *Coping Through the Senses Group.*
- place conducive to learning breathing techniques and practicing meditation.
- place quipped to teach patients about the variety of sensory options that can be used for self-regulation and positive coping strategies.
- place where patients can engage in light exercise or yoga.

SENSORY ROOM RULES

- ✔ Staff must accompany patients.
- ✔ Patient limit is four except for group time.
- ✔ Lock up equipment.
- ✔ Groups must be scheduled ahead of time.
- ✔ Training is mandatory for staff.

Copyright © 2005 Karen M. Moore

Suggestions For Day Room Space

- Check the area for elements that tend to irritate the senses. Look for flickering fluorescent bulbs, wall color that is too strong, spaces that are too crowded, clutter, dark areas, unsafe or uncomfortable furniture, pictures that are too stimulating, etc.

- Add full spectrum lighting; it helps to improve moods.

- Decorate walls and furniture with light, pleasing colors and subtle patterns. Intense colors and striking patterns can be visually exciting to the point of over-stimulation.

- Avoid dark rugs or complex floor patterns that can be confusing to patients with perceptual difficulties and low vision.

- Introduce fine art to the environment. Art can be used to decorate the walls, or books on art can be placed on shelves or on the tables.

- Add music to the environment.

- Decorate for the holidays. This can bring a festive atmosphere, and it can help with orientation to time of year.

- Create a bulletin board collage of photographs of the residents, various activities, friends, families, and pets. It can help start conversations and help patients to learn about one another.

- Provide items that are fun to look at (sun catchers, mobiles, sun activated window chime, aquarium or artificial fish tank).

- Provide items that are fun to smell like hand creams, scented candles (unlit), or occasional spray of a room fragrance.

- Have periodic snacks of fruit or hard candies, herbal teas, or other beverages to stimulate the taste sense.

- Provide rocking chairs or gliders that are comfortable; they can be used by patients who are anxious or upset.

- Offer lap quilts with interesting textures that provide subtle deep pressure touch.

- Keep a basket of current magazines, nature and picture books, and books about animals.

- Provide a basket of stress balls, beanbags, and fidget widgets that patients can experiment with.

- Set up an activity corner with items such as playing cards, games, jig saw puzzles, cross word and word search puzzles, colored pencils and coloring projects, art paper and supplies.

Copyright © 2005 Karen M. Moore

Recommendations For Hospital Environments

Smell: Watch for noxious odors. Use fragrance boxes to form positive associations with smells. Encourage family members to bring in soaps and shampoos with familiar scents.

Taste: Remind caregivers that medications alter taste perceptions. Monitor the impact of illness on nutrition. Use familiar tastes. Encourage family members to bring in favorite snacks and ethnic foods.

Visual: Display personal items and pictures. Post signs. Provide artwork and photography of nature scenes. Use cool colors and simple patterns. Avoid dark or complex patterns on the floor. Use an aquarium or artificial fish tank or other interesting visual sensory input such as a bubble lamp or sun catchers. Decorate with fresh flowers or plants. Have a selection of comedy shows and movie videos.

Auditory: Use music judiciously. Minimize unit noise. Be sensitive to sounds that could trigger flashbacks. Allow patient input into music choices. The music by Mozart is known to be helpful for calming.

Touch: Suggest bringing a quilt or a favorite robe from home. Encourage comfortable clothing. Use weighted lap pads for calming. Provide stress balls and beanbags when appropriate. Tight tuck bed sheets to provide deep pressure touch. Always acquire permission before touching a patient.

Vestibular/Proprioceptive: Provide rocking chairs or gliders. Encourage supervised and judicious use of exercise equipment. Allow room to walk or pace around. Provide a chair exercise tape.

Space: Provide quiet space. Allow a place of retreat for paranoid or overwhelmed patients. Allow adequate personal space, and avoid small closed in rooms with no easy exit.

SAFE SPACE

The amount of time to use the "safe space" is based on each patient's circumstances. Some possible combinations are listed below:

1. **One to two hours following any major disruption or stressful event.**
2. **Planned half-hour times in the morning, afternoon or evening.**
3. **One hour before and after an expected stressful event, outing, or appointment.**
4. **One hour after returning home from work or day program.**

DESIGN A SAFE SPACE

- ✔ Begin with a comfortable chair (rocking chair or glider, if possible) located in a private, quiet space that allows some privacy.

- ✔ Have some things pleasing to look at (landscape scene, photographs, favorite poem, interesting sculpture or figurine, view from a window).

- ✔ Include items to stroke or feel (pet, Koosh ball, stress ball, Chinese iron balls to manipulate, fuzzy something, fidget widget).

- ✔ Provide pleasant products to smell (candles, potpourri, cedar pillow, soaps, lotion).

- ✔ Keep some interesting tastes available (hot balls, fire balls, beef jerky, gum, strong mints, herbal tea).

- ✔ Be sure there is a CD or audiotape player in the room with relaxation tapes (use music that is a little different from what is usually used). Consider a music box.

- ✔ Keep a blanket or throw available.

- ✔ Post a few positive affirmations on the wall ("I am a good person." or "I can't control what happens, but I can control my response" or "I am safe and I can relax." or "I deserve to be pampered").

- ✔ Practice deep breathing when in this space.

- ✔ Use the safe space before and after stressful events or for designated periods in the day.

- ✔ **Do not overuse the safe space.** Educate others to support and respect the need for judicious use of this safe space.

Copyright © 2005 Karen M. Moore

Suggestions To Enrich Home Environments
Give choices! Give control!

Smell/Taste Suggestions
- Avoid chemical and noxious odors
- Provide a variety of scents: candles, potpourri, scented pillows
- Offer scented toiletries: perfume, lotion, cologne, aftershave, bath salts or oils, scented soap, scented powders
- Spritz the room with a fragrant home spray
- Offer tasty treats: spices, fireball candy, sour balls, strong peppermints, ethnic condiments
- Vary diet in taste and texture; watch for oral defensiveness

Auditory Suggestions
- Decrease noise levels, monitor for possible auditory triggers
- Play music that is enjoyable (vary and limit time to avoid it becoming irritating)
- Provide soothing sounds: wind chimes, bubbling fountain or aquarium, music boxes
- Try using repetitive sounds for comfort (white noise): a fan, clock with a loud tick
- Tape and play voices of loved ones and songs of grandchildren
- Use books on tape

Visual Suggestions
- Provide calming visual interest: aquarium, lava lamp, mobile
- Use pleasant pictures, art, decorations, photos of happy times and loved ones
- Place a birdfeeder outside the window for bird watching
- To decrease visual stimulation, wear hooded clothing or wrap around sunglasses
- Decrease clutter
- Consider the use of full spectrum lighting

Touch/Tactile Suggestions
- Assure a comfortable temperature (increase warmth for elderly and ill)
- Offer a heavy coverlet or lap quilt
- Try comforting warmth of a hot water bottle, electric heat pad or blanket, warm packs
- Use soft, non-irritating clothing.
- Try beanbag chairs or throw pillows that wrap around and provide comfort touch
- Make available hand and foot rollers, Chinese iron balls, or beanbags for tapping
- Encourage use of cream for hand or body massage
- Offer back rubs or hugs, hold hands, place a comforting hand on the shoulder
- Provide "Fidget-widgets," stress balls, or Koosh balls to manipulate in hands
- Consider a pet or a "Heavy Duty" realistic stuffed animal

Proprioceptive Suggestions
- Make exercise equipment available if appropriate
- Encourage a walking routine. Set up a walking buddy
- Try an exercise video or chair exercise program
- Offer gum or something safe to chew on
- Arrange attendance at a swimming program, aquacise, Yoga, Tai Chi, or martial arts program

Vestibular Suggestions
- Provide a rocking chair, glider, porch swing, outdoor swing
- Encourage bike riding, car rides

Spatial Suggestions
- Provide a retreat or "safe space"
- Precede and follow difficult excursions with time in a quiet area
- Arrange comfortable seating by a window or place where there is activity to observe

Helping Patients With Cognitive Deficits

- Post important numbers by the phone where they are clearly visible. Have the patient practice calling important numbers.

- Display a calendar in a central location of the house. Mark appointments, events, & special days on it.

- Develop a routine for checking the calendar, such as immediately after breakfast.

- Put a large clock in a place that is highly visible. Hourly chimes are helpful.

- Set paper and pencils by the phone for messages.

- Encourage the patient to write down any appointments or plans for the day.

- Help the patient to establish the habit of always placing things in the same spot such as keys or slippers or an address book.

- Do not hurry to replace old things with new ones as the patient may not recognize them.

- Set the radio to a favorite channel and tape the button in that place.

- Set up night-lights and at least one light that turns on automatically at dusk.

- Use well-marked medication strips and leave med containers in a visible location. Throw out any old medications. Clean out the medicine cabinet.

- Put out clean clothes for the patient to see them. Keep clothing choices simple.

- Use coat trees and coat hooks for sweaters and robes and frequently worn clothing. Put toothbrushes, soaps, deodorants, and other toiletries in plain sight on the vanity.

- Put sunscreen and boots and umbrellas by the door.

- Post a list by the door of things to check before going out: check stove, turn off hall light, and lock all doors.

- If a patient's living space needs to be relocated, set up necessary items and furniture as closely as possible to the former arrangement.

- Use pastel colors and uncomplicated patterns to minimize excitability and confusion. Cut down on clutter. Remove any unnecessary furniture or rugs. Simplify decorations.

- Make the bathroom safe with grab bars and non-slip pads and a shower stool.

- If a patient is unsafe around the stove, unplug it and make other arrangements for hot meals.

- Keep cabinets and refrigerator stocked with essential items only.

- Remove unsafe equipment including coffee makers, electric knives, and electric appliances.

- Designate a box or shelf for all bills and important mail and arrange for help for money management. Give the patient daily allowances for money.

- Establish pre-set times and routines for leisure participation and socialization.

Copyright © 2005 Karen M. Moore